by **SPENCER**

GRENDAHL

A FIRESIDE BOOK
PUBLISHED BY SIMON & SCHUSTER INC.
NEW YORK LONDON TORONTO SYDNEY TOKYO

ROMANCE On

PALMISTRY
for LOVERS

YOUR HANDS

Fireside
Simon & Schuster Building
Rockefeller Center
1230 Avenue of the Americas
New York, New York 10020
Copyright © 1990 by J. Spencer Grendahl

Designed by Bonni Leon

Manufactured in the United States of America
1   3   5   7   9   10   8   6   4   2
Library of Congress Cataloging in Publication Data
Grendahl, Spencer.
Romance on your hands : palmistry for lovers / by Spencer
Grendahl.
p.   cm.
1. Palmistry.   2. Love.   3. Mate selection.   I. Title.
BF935.L67G74 1990
133.6—dc20   89-29527
CIP
ISBN 0-671-68098-6

To all
grandmothers
and their
spiritual
gifts

ACKNOWLEDGMENTS

More than my hand made this book a reality. I want to thank Sherry Robb for representing me; Barbara Gess for taking this project and this writer under her wing; and Cindy Lao, whose efforts often went above and beyond the call of duty. Other helpers include Sue Price for her intuition and encouragement, "Mim" Eichler for her word-processing and editorial skills, and Susan Wilder for her sure hand on the graphics. Thanks have to go to the literally thousands of individuals whose palms I have read in the last twenty years. And finally, my gratitude to the spiritual presence of Grandmother Harris, whose way of life was the most profound book one could ever read.

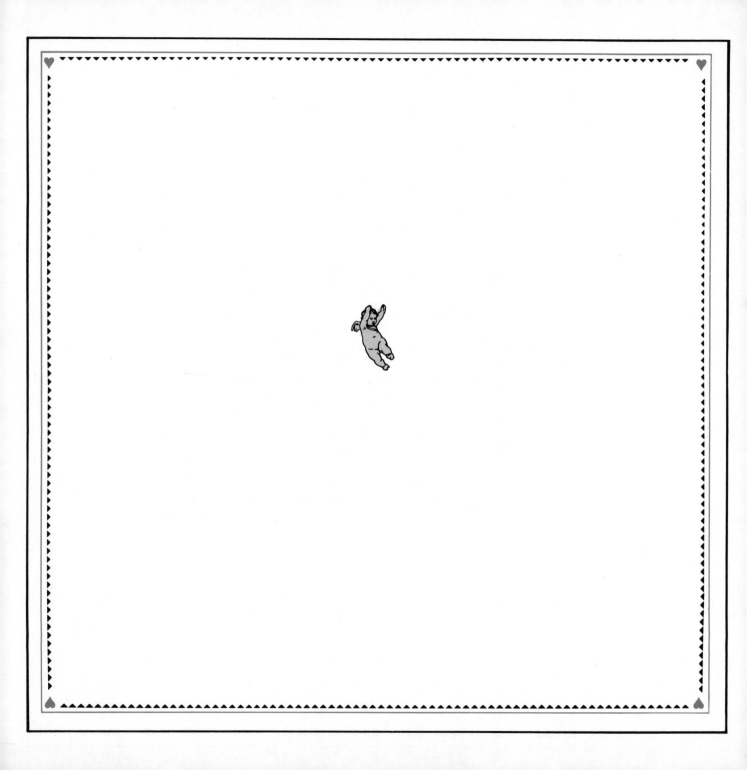

CONTENTS

LIST OF ILLUSTRATIONS

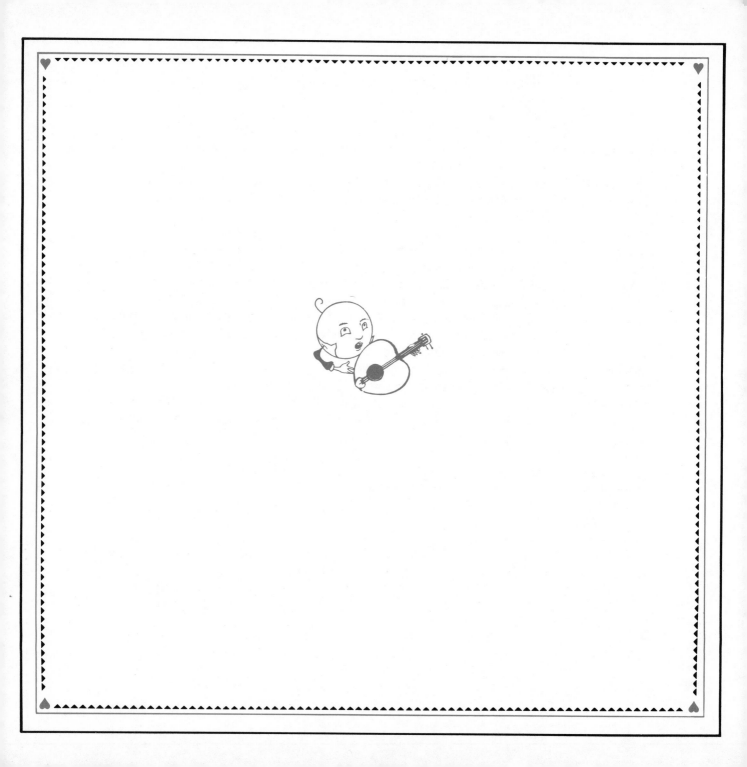

PREFACE

A palmist! This little old lady was telling me that I would be a palmist! It was in my hand, she announced enthusiastically. Concentrating on my palm as if it were a Chinese hexagram, she turned through the pages of my life as if it were an open book. Despite my cynicism, I was intrigued. How could this happen?

The reader was Grandmother Harris. She was eighty-two; I was nineteen. That fateful hand reading on a crisp fall morning began a friendship that would last over eleven years, until her death. Actually she wasn't my grandmother, but the grandmother of my girlfriend, Joan. Joan and I had gone to her parents' home for one of those "girl's family meets the boyfriend" weekends, an awkward situation at best. Meeting Grandmother changed my life—not instantly, but in a slow, sure way, as her life of the spirit became my way of life.

Joan had told me that her Grandmother Harris was quite a palmist and had for years been active in many metaphysical and spiritualist circles. I considered myself a bright, serious student of "deep" literature. I thought I would just humor this kindly old lady.

After brunch, Grandmother Harris asked to read my palm. Only with my consent did she carefully take my hands and begin to look at their shape, at my fingers and thumb, touching various points. "You know," she started, "you will be a fine palmist. You have the double mystic cross, and look here, Neptune's Fork on the Mount of Jupiter, the ambition to know the unknown." I was unconvinced by all this psychic prattle. Then she shifted gears. "You are very creative, you can write, you can talk. One of your lessons in life will be to feel. You distrust feelings. Feelings have hurt you." This struck me deeply, for it was true. My father had died when I was fifteen and I had clammed up after that. I joked that Joan must have given a good background report on me, but it wasn't so. The lady could read hands!

Grandmother Harris and I hit it off. Something about her spirit, her inner being, could not be suppressed. She beamed forth some kind of magnetic charm that, despite my sophomoric seriousness, drew me closer and closer to the core of her warmth. Before Joan and I left her house, Grandmother Harris gave me a palmistry book and my first lesson, the importance of noting exactly how you feel when you first touch a person's hand. And as we were about to go out the door, she smiled at us and said, "You children are going to be the greatest of friends."

Joan and I never married, but we remain very good friends, and from that first meeting Grandmother Harris and I became avid correspondents. She always answered the questions in my letters with hope and insight.

Often, in elderly women there is great wisdom. Like the Earth Mother, their nature is to foster regeneration and growth. The sagacity of such seasoned women can heal the fallow mind and cause it to bloom again. To my surprise, I started studying palmistry, first out of curiosity to see how it worked, and later with disciplined determination, getting all the lessons I could by corresponding with Grandmother Harris and visiting her personally when possible. Years later when I was living in Los Angeles and becoming a professional, I met the famous Singapore palmist, Joachim Bennet, at a palmistry class he was teaching. He informed me that whoever had taught me had done an excellent job.

My career as a professional palm reader did not start until years after my initial lessons with Grandmother Harris. Somehow most people, myself included, do not start life thinking about becoming a professional palmist. One becomes a professional by a simple twist of fate. Necessity knocks, and the door must be opened. This was the case with me.

Thanks to Grandmother Harris, I was a good amateur reader, amazing my friends and others with my skills. But my level of expertise was limited by my narrow frame of experience. This all changed in Los Angeles, where I met the West Coast editor of *VIVA* Magazine, Toni Biggs, who was impressed with my palmistry skills. This led to my writing a series of palmistry articles for *VIVA* and becoming a professional palmist.

Quickly the spiritual circuits in L.A. opened up to me. I started to meet celebrities as well as party and event planners, agents who provide services to hostesses who give lots of parties. I found myself giving private readings as well as being asked to give demonstrations at parties. The result of this apprenticeship has been the opportunity to see literally thousands of hands, to listen to countless stories, to be in the very heart of a lot of action as far as palmistry is concerned. As a consequence, it dawned on me that I was in a position to enhance the collective knowledge of palmistry by writing a book drawing on my experiences and personal insights. I wanted it to be about relationships, for I think palmistry is most rewarding in understanding love.

Over the years, the largest concern of all the people whose hands I've read is to know if their love will last, if they are right for each other. Predictably many couples will come to me and ask if they are compatible. I will compare their palms and make my comments. "How do you know so much about us?" is their first response. "Could you teach me to do that?" usually follows.

This book, *Romance on Your Hands*, was written in response to all the wonderful people who have asked me questions about love and have shown me their hands. I have learned a great deal from their honest evaluations of my remarks about their compatibility needs, and I'd like to pass that knowledge on to you.

These basic principles of palmistry can open up a whole new world, a different perspective with new vistas. This knowledge can be used not only as a tool to evaluate your compatibility with a love interest, but as a springboard for connecting with new people you meet. Starting a conversation about the lines of the hand is a pleasant icebreaker for deeper discussion.

Palmistry is fun, so have fun with this book. The one concept Grandmother Harris taught above all else is that a positive approach always gets the best results. See the good in people and the good in them will come out for you!

Now it is your turn to study and enjoy, as the human race has for thousands of years, the mystery of the lines on the hand. This book is as clear for the beginner as I could make it. Try its lessons and principles with openness and candor! You'll be just as amazed as I was that fateful day Grandmother Harris first taught me the language of palmistry, and the lines on the hand began to speak to me.

INTRODUCTION: GETTING STARTED

What is palmistry?

Palmistry is a way of interpreting the shape of the hand and the lines of the palm so that the character and possible life experiences of an individual can be projected or "read." There is no need to be psychic—though it helps to be sensitive or intuitive. The language of the hand can be read by anyone who knows the simple alphabet of lines and shapes. Once fluent in the alphabet of classic palmistry, new vistas and horizons of personal insight open up. Just seeing a hand for a moment—catching a glimpse of its lines and structure—can bring enormous revelations that may prove invaluable in work, love, and socializing.

Why are lines so important? How can we know so much by paying attention to them? Many people think that the lines on the hand are simply flexure lines, lines caused by the way the hand creases when it opens and closes. This isn't true.

The modern theory is that the lines of the hand represent a graphic shorthand of the circuits of the brain. Recent medical work, reported in *Time* and *Newsweek*, has supported this view on the significance of the hand's lines. The nerve group that controls the hands is exactly in the center of the brain, and all the electrical energies of our thinking pass through it. Palmists and this growing number of medical authorities feel that the lines on the hand form in some relationship to thought patterns, nerve linkages, or even chromosomal structures in this central hand/nerve group and reflect traits of the whole mental structure.

I once had the opportunity to read palms at the party of a famous surgeon. The party was filled with surgeons who presumed that my services were engaged for the sole entertainment of their wives. As the evening wore on, however, the doctors themselves started coming over for readings and I asked them what they thought caused the differences in the lines on the hand. Many had no opinion, but several believed that the differences had something to do with nerve endings in the palm.

One hand specialist and I struck up a friendship. This man was a marvel of needle and thread who had been known to sew people's hands back together after terrible accidents. He was convinced that the nerves of the hand cause the variations of lines. He explained that when nerves that go to the hand are severed, the hand loses its lines. He asserted that his opinions and experiences, both personal and scientific, seemed to lend credence to the palmist's contention that the lines of the hand are a blueprint of the neurological make-up of the individual. This theory may also explain how the lines of the hand can change when a person's behavior changes.

The question raised is: which came first, the personality change or the change in the line on the hand? The answer is most certainly that the personality change happens first. The will and the mind change first and the lines follow to reflect those changes. The tail does not wag the dog, does it? If you change your thinking, your mental motivation, your willful intent, then this new attitude and mindful shift is manifested in changes in the lines on your hand. Unfortunately, some people don't change, so their lines remain static and unchanging. Alternatively, I have witnessed major alterations in people's hands that mirrored dramatic personal transformations. Superficial changes will not manifest in the line changes; only a true change in thinking will appear.

When approaching a person's hands, place the most importance on the dominant hand, secondary importance on the subdominant. It is the dominant hand you write with, because writing is a direct expression of the personality. The dominant is the hand in control, the one that signs checks. So you will read the right hand of a right-handed person and the left hand of a left-handed person. The dominant hand reflects the rational mind, while the subdominant hand reveals the emotional mind.

Does this mean that you overlook the subdominant altogether? For most purposes and to insure accuracy, all you have to do is look quickly at the two hands of your lover—or prospective lover—and see if the two appear to be of relatively equal shape and similar line markings. Most people do have similar configurations, so in these cases you need only look to the dominant hand.

However, if the subdominant hand has lines which appear stronger, more wildly structured, or radically different, you must consider this hand as a powerful source of emotional input. Make note of its strength, which is sure to test the rational awareness and control of the personality. Be sure to notice if the thumb or fingers differ in length or shape; a major difference between thumbs or index fingers can reveal an imbalance in will or logic that can be a problem for this person. Examine any differences in line markings in reference to whatever area of life shows up as important on the dominant hand. Conflicts in emotional or rational themes for this individual should be identified and studied.

If you find such differences in the major palm lines, in the shape of the hands, or in their bone structure, you'll need to look up both types of lines or finger patterns in the diagrams of this book. Remember, this is necessary only when you see measurable differences. By looking up the meanings of the different elements, you'll be able to understand the type of personality factors or conflicts that are at work between the "right and left brains" of this individual. Observe the persona and see how the various components do or do not contribute to problems. Please don't announce, "Wow, are you in conflict! The lines of your right and left hand are at war. They're running you ragged." You will not win a friend and you will miss getting to know this person. These differences can be dynamic indeed, and sometimes destructive, but any conclusions you make must be reached quietly and patiently, and not until you have exhaustively studied all the elements at hand.

THE BASIC ELEMENTS

Palmistry is divided into two broad areas: the study of hand structure or cheirology, and the study of the lines of the palm, or cheiromancy. Since you usually see the whole hand first, let's begin with the basic hand shapes. You can start practicing palmistry immediately and privately, just by examining people's hand shapes and gaining speedy new insights. Here are some basic concepts you'll need before getting down to work. We'll be returning to these concepts in greater detail once you have mastered this simple alphabet.

There are five basic hand types: realistic, receptive, analytical, active, and mixed.

The *realistic hand* is square or sharply rectangular, with square fingertips and smooth or slightly developed knuckles on the fingers. The flesh is muscular, pinkish, firm to very hard. The mentality is practical, dogmatic, materialistic.

The *receptive hand* appears roundish with lots of soft flesh on a rectangular palm. The fingers are delicate with conic tips—pointed to slightly pointed—and smooth knuckles. The palm is spongy to the touch, sometimes moist. These individuals can pick up the vibrations of thought and emotions.

The *analytical hand* is very bony, both rectangular and narrow, with flat, firm, dry flesh, and sinuous, taut muscles. The strongest identifying characteristics are large knuckles on skinny fingers. This is the hand of the critic.

The *active hand* is rectangular or slightly trapezoidal in shape with firm muscular flesh and a sharply resilient feeling to the touch. The fingers are smooth to slightly knuckled, with rectangular or trapezoidal tips. This is nervous energy in action.

The *mixed hand* is a combination of the qualities of two or more of these four basic types. Most often the mix is of one type of fingers combined with a second type of palm—active fingers on a realistic palm, for example. Here is a person who can get things done quickly in a realistic manner and who also knows when it's time to relax. We'll take a deeper look at other combinations farther on.

FINGERS AND THUMBS

The fingers are named for the gods of classical Greek and Roman mythology. The index finger is known as Jupiter, the middle finger as Saturn, the ring finger as Apollo, and the little finger or pinky as Mercury. The thumb is called Rhea. Each will fall into a classification of realistic (meaty and square-tipped); receptive (fleshy with smooth knuckles and conic tips); analytical (bony with defined knuckles, square or slightly rounded tips); or active (sinuous with slight knuckle and trapezoidal tips). A single finger can be mixed as well (analytical knuckles with receptive tips—a supersensitive critic), but only in rare cases. More common is a mixture of different types of fingers on a hand—perhaps three realistic fingers and one active, or a thumb of one basic type and the fingers of another. The latter would imply that the individual's will, as seen in the thumb, is different in nature from the fingers' capacity to act. A receptive thumb, for example, combined with active fingers, would indicate someone who might not be strong in getting work done, but might anticipate or sense issues of the task that others can not see. There would also be a lack of competitiveness with such a combination; the receptive thumb would shy away from criticism and scatter into emotionalism.

Knowing even a bit of the mythology that inspired the naming of the fingers with their associated personality characteristics and life themes, along with the classifications that we have just reviewed, will enhance the artistry of your readings. Many of the following key phrases also describe the mounts of the hand, which we'll explore in a moment.

Jupiter, the index finger. This is the finger of leadership, of adventure, of ego strength. Long—domineering. Medium—gracious authority. Short—advisory; more following than leading. Crooked—very animated and active.

Saturn, middle finger. This is the finger of discretion, or prudence, of planning and balance. Long—extremely cautious. Medium—moderate and discreet. Short—morally facile. Crooked—overly conscientious.

Apollo, ring finger. This is the finger of discernment, of romance and style. Long—extreme in taste and style. Medium—balanced, tasteful. Short—leaning toward mainstream style and taste. Crooked—leaning toward moral taste.

Mercury, little finger. This is the finger of communication, of conversational or written skills, of coordination. Long—a born salesperson. Medium—honest and forthright. Short—withholds information or is shy. Crooked—will bend words to get what is desired.

Rhea, the thumb. This is the phalanges of the will. It opposes the fingers, and this opposition makes things happen. Long—the will is very strong, possibly stubborn. Medium—the will is strong, yet able to negotiate in give-and-take situations. Short—has difficulty sustaining a long effort.

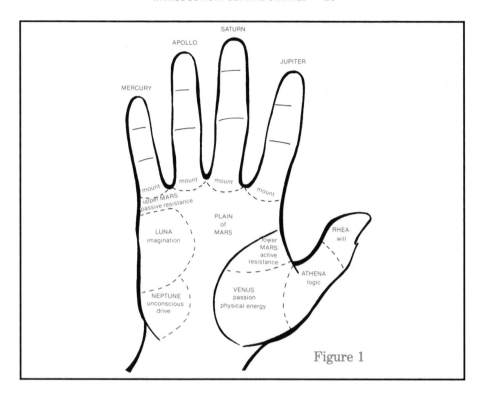

Figure 1

MOUNTS

As you can see in figure 1, there is a "mount" under each finger, a padded area which can be either a high mount—a little rounded hill of flesh—or a flat mount, a subtle plateau. The mount contributes to the strength of the finger, as its physiological function is to pad the finger joint to the palm.

High mounts indicate sharp, sensuous energy and an active, physical personality. For example, Jupiter with a high mount signals someone with a heightened desire to rule or control, to be the one in a leadership position.

Low plateau mounts add mental energy to the type of finger. Jupiter with a low mount would therefore indicate someone who wants to rule with ideas.

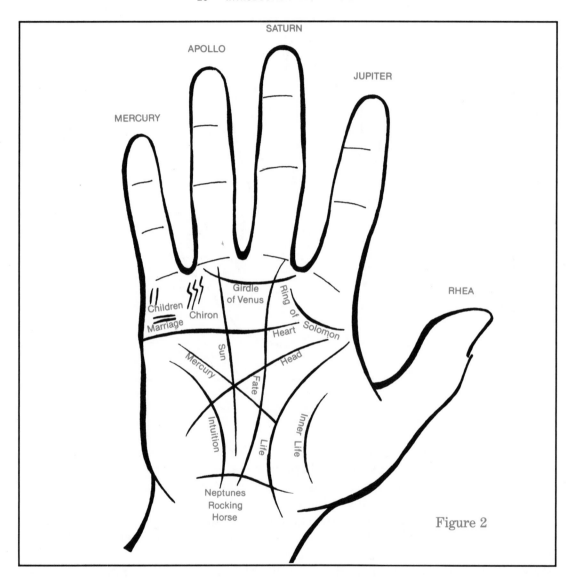

Figure 2

THE MAJOR LINES

There are three major lines of the hand—the Line of Life, the Line of Head, and the Line of Heart. These three major lines, along with the finger types and the palm classifications, are collectively considered the "basic five." You'll soon be comparing and scoring these basic five components for compatibility in the arena of love. The map of the hand (figure 2) highlights these lines and can be used as a reference throughout this book.

The *Line of Life* circles the thumb, starting at the base of the Mount of Jupiter—or below the index finger—and running around the Mount of Venus, the muscle at the base of the palm under the thumb. The Line of Life represents the vitality of the individual. A strong Line of Life runs long and deep, giving robust health and powerful energies. If the line is shallow, the individual has difficulty sustaining efforts in competition. A short line does not signify early death, but a point at which psychological or spiritual growth halts. This can change as lines grow and develop.

The *Line of Head* runs from the edge of the Line of Life into the center of the palm or onto the Plain of Mars. Straight lines indicate a practical, though somewhat inflexible outlook. Curved lines mean a creative and flexible attitude. A long Line of Head is a mark of someone who can deal in abstract thought; those with short lines like the real world and are usually doers of all kinds.

The *Line of Heart* runs along the base of the fingers, just under the mounts. A straight Heart Line is found on one who controls his emotions. A curved Heart Line reveals an extrovert, someone who can express feelings spontaneously. If it's long, it indicates someone with intense emotions; if short, the individual may distance himself psychologically from emotions.

DEVELOPING YOUR OWN STYLE

Every metaphysical reader has a personal style, and I encourage you to develop yours at the outset. From the first observation you make about a hand you see— even in passing—allow yourself to respond in your own personal way. I suggest that you first clear your mind by taking a couple of relaxing breaths before touching the hand you are about to examine. Feel the hand with your intuitive sense when you first touch it. Note your reaction to the hand, its temperature, dryness, or moistness, any trait that stands out. You may get a feeling that the person is sad, happy, afraid, lonely, tired, anxious. Just take those feelings in and note them. As you move along with your examination of the hand, these first impressions will be very helpful in getting a fix on that person. It is common, for example, for a person with a long straight Line of Heart to show intensity. If you are reading a short straight Line of Heart and the person seems tense, you know that he or she is preoccupied with a pressing issue. Use your personal judgment in deciding if and how you should mention or help with that problem.

DON'T BE A CASSANDRA OF DOOM

I cannot emphasize enough what tremendous power you can have when giving a palmistry reading. During the reading your subject may be filled with superstition, fear, dread. I once was asked to read at a party, but I could not attend because of a previous engagement. Instead, I gave the hostess the name of a reader whom, although I had heard of him, I had never met. Later the hostess called to let me know that this reader had ruined her party by forecasting illness, death, divorce, and financial loss. The reader was destructive, and used the power of palmistry negatively. This is not to say that awful things never come to pass; sadly they do. Still, a party is hardly a place to start talking about death. And what's more, it's very difficult to predict bad news with accuracy, so why try? As one of my students has said, "Be a perk, not a jerk."

Another client of mine was told by a palm reader that he would get cancer at age forty-seven. From that moment on, he lived with a secret fear that the prediction would come true. I could not for the life of me find the clues to the cancer prediction on his hand. I'm pleased to announce that my client is now fifty-three, and has never had cancer. That prediction was completely inaccurate; yet look at the fear it caused! This example illustrates the power of the palm reader—even the most hardened cynic can secretly worry over a terrible pronouncement.

Please use the information in this book to be positive, to look for the good sides of the person whose hand you are reading or whom you are considering as a mate. If there aren't many positives to this person, remain silent and withdraw politely. Be thorough in your readings, as you may have overlooked a wonderful trait that was right under your nose. If you err in a reading, err on the side of good—always give the person the benefit of the doubt and watch the individual actually improve. The greatest aspect of our dawning New Age is its upbeat, positive metaphysical direction.

Fate versus free will is an issue that always comes up. People will ask you, "Am I destined to live out the lines on my hand?" The answer is always, "No, you are not." The lines reflect mental and neurological make-up. As we discussed earlier, the lines can change. People are able to change their lives and thereby change their lines. It is unfortunate that many seem stuck in their ruts of daily habit and seldom exercise free will. We will return to this profound issue in our final chapter.

HOW TO USE THIS BOOK

Skim through Part One, "Five Ways to Read Your Lover," to get an overview, and then read carefully each of the following sections at your own pace: Hand Shapes, Fingers, Line of Life, Line of Head, and Line of Heart. Take the time to mull over the concepts, to compare your hands and others' to the diagrams given as examples. Test the concepts of compatibility on your dates, friends, new people you meet. After this, you can continue to use this book as a reference, though you will probably have already absorbed the important concepts. Until you feel fluent in the language, you may wish to consult frequently the basic maps of the hand shown at the end of this chapter.

Mastering the evaluation system detailed at the end of the basic five section should not be difficult, but do give yourself plenty of practice. Play with the broader ideas and soon you will be able to make quick, specific judgments that follow from the easy steps of the system. You can evaluate not only your own compatibility needs in relationships, but also how other couples may or may not match up.

Continue, then, to augment your blossoming abilities by studying the sections on the minor lines—Saturn or the Line of Fate, the Line of Sun, the Lines of Marriage, Intuition, and Neptune. Knowledge of the minor lines will fine-tune your skills and insights. Play with these ideas and develop your own dialogue—how the lines speak to you.

Return when necessary to this section for a refresher course on the bare bones of palm-reading theory and the basic maps of the hand. This will be your foundation of knowledge. From here on, let your own style blossom forth as we flesh out those bare bones.

I laud you in your discovery of *Romance on Your Hands* and welcome you as a new or continuing student of palmistry. Properly used, the material presented in this book will set off a process that allows you to tap into the artistry of palm reading. It is possible to teach techniques or other scientific methodologies, but teaching art is a different matter. Palmistry is an art based upon the features of the hand—it is therefore not altogether a precise science. It is an expression, an alphabet of a language that you can learn to speak, practice, and enjoy in your own way. I remember watching the late great palmist Sydney Rushakoff of Los Angeles as he was working. He had a grand style, with a fine use of language, a feeling for the spirit and a positive emphasis that drew people to him. He and I worked together one evening and he told me, "See through the hand to the soul, Spencer." It is the same advice I now give you. Good luck!

PART ♥ ONE

FIVE WAYS to READ YOUR LOVER

The hand shapes, fingers and thumb, the Line of Life, Line of Head, and Line of Heart are the five basic elements of palmistry. Analyzing these major hand characteristics will give you strong insights when evaluating your lover's potential as a partner in a serious relationship. At the end of Part One, you will find an easy-to-use chart to help you add up the plusses and minuses seen in the hands.

A new relationship is an exciting adventure. Hopefully, the information from the ancient art of palmistry will shed a clear and stimulating light on the topography of your love life.

1

THE SHAPES of THE HAND

Understanding the significance of the shape of the hand is the first step in becoming fluent in the language of palmistry. As we've already seen, there are four basic hand types and there are six mixtures of these types. Again, the four fundamental types are: receptive, realistic, active, and analytical. Other palmists list as many as seven hand types (such as conic, square, or spatulate), but I have condensed them to the above four types for greater clarity and easier learning; the mixed type will be discussed as an adjunct. Some palmists identify hand types according to the four classical elements of fire, water, earth, and air. The trouble with this method is that students always get confused as to what, for example, an "air" hand is. Unless they are trained in the metaphysics of Aristotle, few modern students think in terms of these "classic elements" of air, water, earth, and fire.

The method presented here has proved to be reliable and sensible with countless palmistry students. With minimum assessment, hands can be quickly judged: realistic, active, receptive, or analytical. Simple "key" phrases will help you identify the hand types.

This classification system makes it equally easy to discern the mixtures of these four types. The analytical-receptive mixture, for example, is easier for many students to understand than an "air-water" hand.

The classification of hand shapes is an aspect of palmistry that should not be quickly passed over in favor of the more dramatic line reading. Many students are eager to skip the basics and go directly to studying lines, but the meanings of the lines are deeply influenced by the shape of the hand. In fact, the hand shape functions as an identifiable energy pattern or psychic filter through which the life-force passes. Therefore a line of intuition on a realistic hand may only indicate strong hunches, whereas on the receptive hand this line may signal significant extrasensory perception.

A romantic Heart Line on an active hand will often manifest as a thousand romantic deeds, a scatter-gun effect. On the analytical hand, however, it will often mean that the person chooses the way he expresses his romantic feelings very carefully. This expression will bear the mark of consideration, thinking and rethinking, and finally a great seriousness. These individuals play for keeps.

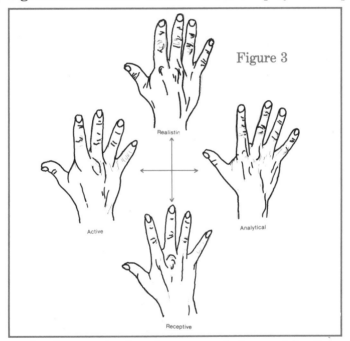

Figure 3

Figure 3 shows the four major hand types and the combinations that can occur. Consider each major type to be a kingdom or region on a map, each having its own government, national personality, emotional currency rates, and psychological weather. Knowing the philosophy of each "realm," of each hand type, you will be better prepared to understand the person.

♥ THE REALISTIC HAND ♥

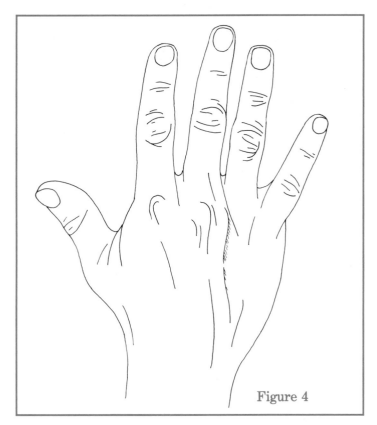

Figure 4

KEYS

SQUARE OR
RECTANGULAR PALM ♥
SQUARE FINGERTIPS ♥
SMOOTH TO SLIGHT
KNUCKLES ON FINGERS
VITAL,
MUSCULAR,
HARD, OR
FIRM FLESH

The realistic hand (figure 4) is usually easy to spot by its square or slightly rectangular shape and square-shaped fingers. The knuckles may be smooth or slightly knotty. The palm is close to being equal in length and width, and is usually moderately stiff to quite stiff in flexibility. The hand is very firm in texture, even hard sometimes, a solid piece of flesh, a hunk of earth, even stone.

Skin varies from very coarse to moderately fine. Line formations range from the extremely simple (just three major lines) to a high degree of complexity. Still, of all the types of hands, this type can often have the fewest lines. Palmists of the older schools call the simple realistic palm the "elemental hand" because it has only a palm and three lines. In actuality, this simple configuration represents only the first level of a whole group of realistic types.

Realistic hand types are very resourceful and can deal with life as it is. They have determination, drive, and follow-through. Since they are so well grounded, they understand time, are patient, and have good timing in practical matters. They live in the here-and-now and are not about to be led off on some childish crusade.

This hand can be quite precise. Like surgeons or engineers, these people can do things with tools, instruments, and wires. This gives them an instinctive streak, especially in mechanical or electrical areas. They are the ones who always know what broke in the car ("I'll just bet the fan belt went out"). They are productive and confident; they know what they are working for and what they can get out of it.

People with realistic hands are very consistent. They recognize that repetition is what enables a lot of things to happen: go to work each day, work hard, get a raise. This makes them dependable, but also makes them susceptible to ruts—they'll often eat the same foods all the time, shop at the same stores, and go to the same restaurants.

There is a strong sense of method in this type. They know that the field is plowed one furrow at a time, the wall is built one brick at a time, and the toaster can often be fixed by plugging it in.

This group is often wise with investments. They know that money is a real commodity that should be managed and invested safely to make more money. Don't be surprised if they long to own real estate or blue-chip stock. Realistic types are adamant about dependable returns on their hard cash. They're quick to size up and reject what might be a fly-by-night investment proposition.

Here is a solid personality, one that can take criticism and deal with others pragmatically. Not at all moody, they're very often balanced in their day-to-day emotions. In terms of personal growth, they will acknowledge that there is always room for improvement. After all, being realistic means not letting any good opportunity to improve slip by.

Realistic types avoid the liberal arts, and lean toward science and the measurable, that which can be perceived objectively. They scoff at highly ethereal subjects and consider spiritualism little more than a joke. They won't hide their opinions—what you see in them is what you get!

As lovers, those with realistic hands are sensual. They love the feel of their lover's skin, the smell, the taste, the pleasure of skin touching skin. These individuals will work to please in lovemaking, but their routine ways may not allow for variation and may get boring. Often they fall into the rut of the same old position, same old gifts, same old music, same words of affection. However, when it comes to endurance, these folks get top scores. They build a fire and keep it going. They can also give great back rubs.

The realistic personality makes for a valuable friend who can see things the way they really are. On the strong side, these individuals can use their grounded point of view to offer genuinely helpful advice that will prove useful down the road. In the poorly developed personality, however, this trait can turn an individual into a spoiler, one who uses realism to destroy other people's dreams. They will blast your plans to pieces with cheap shots.

♥ THE RECEPTIVE HAND ♥

The receptive hand (figure 5) feels soft, spongy, as if your fingers can knead the flesh like dough. While the hands are supported by the bones, it takes time to find them because of the abundance of spongy tissue. The palm looks oval, not because of the bone structure—which is rectangular—but because the flesh rises so high near the Mounts of Venus, Luna, and Neptune.

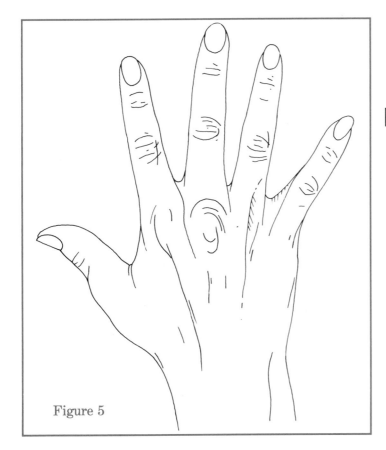

Figure 5

KEYS

ROUNDISH,
RECTANGULAR PALM ♥
CONIC FINGERS ♥
SMOOTH JOINTS ♥
SOFT, SPONGY
FLESH,
SOMETIMES MOIST

The fingers appear thick at the base and then taper down to either tightly rounded or conic tips. These are not really fingers but antennae, fingers that can pick up vibrations, that know what's going on. These fingers are smooth-jointed and indicate a variety of talents. Being so sensitive gives one a lot to respond to, to tune in to; it's like being hooked up and "cable ready."

There is a magnetic quality to these hands. Strong, healing feelings can actually be generated. These individuals can be very calming when they want to be and are the kind of people who seem to attract personal confessions from others. I once suggested to a client that with her receptive type of hands she may well have been a natural healer in a past life. And she agreed with me! She had feelings about the power of her hands for as long as she could remember. She was a natural in calming crying children and was able to have a positive influence on the sick and elderly. When she touched them, they felt definite energy—a peaceful, relaxing force. You would love to let these receptive hands touch you.

Many great spiritual leaders have this type of hand. They are charismatic orators, speaking from a gut level of emotion that achieves results. These people can make their intentions seem so strong, so rooted in passion, as to be undeniable.

Receptives are very discriminating in whatever they do. They insist on having the best wines, cheeses, and exotic cuisines. These folks are sometimes found to be overweight because they love to eat, and they eat good food. Their discriminating outlooks are also evident in other walks of life, in literature, music, and all the creature comforts—such as the type of bed they'll own, what chair they'll sit in, and all the other details of their surroundings.

These people are moody; they can get cranky suddenly and then just as quickly change that mood and turn happy. They can use their sensitivity to be incredibly kind and wonderful to you. But by the same token, they know exactly where to put the needle if they are so inclined.

Receptive individuals do not appreciate criticism. They are "thin-skinned" and take everything personally. While you may think that you are simply talking about a way to improve a skill they have, they'll view your remarks as a personal attack. In short, they take criticism like a balloon takes a pinprick—with a bang, not with a whimper.

The receptive is very passionate but also insecure in love. A wonderfully intuitive partner, this person will tend to be supportive, helpful, aware of what you need as well as the many different ways to give you love and attention. Beware, though. Jealousy can rear its head as the receptive's imagination easily goes into overdrive with even the slightest provocation. But with assurance and education, they can learn to trust and not be paranoid about losing love.

Physically, these individuals are very exciting lovers. Their sensitivity is great, and they aren't afraid to experiment. Their touch is as gentle as a moth's wing fluttering on your skin. Intuition seems to guide them to do exactly what it is that you want.

It is in the realm of romance that receptives are most powerful. They love to anticipate and to build feelings, to develop a relationship mentally so that the electricity just keeps charging. Their attention to little things keeps the romance alive and glowing—a constant fuel to the fire.

The developed aesthetics of the receptive can turn romance into a fine art. They also make a romance out of art, as they are so sensitive to color, tone, texture, and taste that they fall in and out of love with whatever connects to their senses. They are like human thermostats. Receptives are great artists, great performers, and great chefs. Given their moodiness, they personify the temperamental "artiste" in all that they do.

Receptives have a very psychic hand, a ready seismograph of what is going to happen. They pick up vibrations and receive wavelengths. At times, they will appear to read your mind, to read the minds of others, to know who's going to get what and when, to offhandedly make predictions that come to pass. This is a wonderful skill when properly utilized. The paranoid side of this, however, can be manifested when these individuals imagine that negative things are about to happen for no discernible reasons. They may fear that someone is out to get them, or out to get you. When this dark side of the psychic experience emerges, the receptive needs grounding and a trip to a good mineral bath.

♥ THE ACTIVE HAND ♥

Look out, here comes the competitive challenger, *the active hand* (figure 6). This smooth, firm hand with smooth fingers and rounded tips is strong, muscular, not too broad, and not too narrow. It differs from the realistic hand in that it is not as square, it's more flexible, and it doesn't have even a little knot at the knuckles.

KEYS

SQUARE TO
RECTANGULAR PALM
SMOOTH FINGERS
ROUND
FINGERTIPS
FIRM, VITAL,
MUSCULAR FLESH

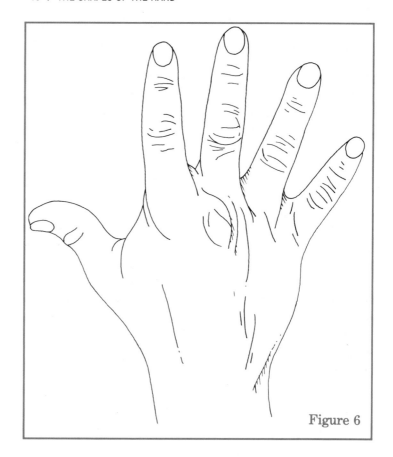

Figure 6

There is a warmth to this hand, and it is usually bright in color.

A very dynamic individual, the active person is confident and enthusiastic, eager to set things in motion. These folks can be quite purposeful and directed. "Do it now!" is their cry.

Power is the great love of the active hand. A natural leader, this person knows that with power a leader can achieve something, create bold new plans, move the opposition, and obtain substantial results.

Very independent, the active types could be called self-centered; their main interest is often how to get ahead. Their competitive spirit is legendary. Others might even conclude that they are self-obsessed. Actives expect everyone else to share their competitive zeal and drive. They may tend to alienate those they are trying to lead by being too pushy and demanding. "We'll work overtime and get it done, tonight, even if we have to work until dawn," an active might say to a colleague, presuming that the co-worker shares the same determination. You'll find the active personality in its element in marketing jobs of any kind, in the love of travel, adventure, and new horizons.

These individuals can, unfortunately, easily become too active. They can mistake motion itself for progress. Often impulsive, they need to be grounded or anchored to ensure that they have their wagon hitched to a star . . . and not to a comet!

Burnout can be a problem for people who have active hands, as it is a natural consequence of trying to do too much too quickly. I had a client at one time who was so frantic to make his small business grow that he exhausted himself and nearly lost the fruit of his labors. In fact it was his wife—who has a realistic hand—who saved him and his business.

The active hand is decisive. Natural executives, actives make up their minds quickly, readily moving on to other matters. They're wonderfully creative in technological fields, in management, and in artistic areas. One client of mine who has an active hand is both an excellent chiropractor and a painter, displaying innovation in both fields.

There is a strong political side to the active person. These individuals like to be involved, to discuss and take positions on the issues. As they are often inspiring speakers, you'll find many toastmasters in this category.

Versatile is the key word for these folks. Scientists and artists alike may have this hand. I've seen active hands on doctors who use the most creative methods in their practice, on lawyers who know more than one way to present ideas to their clients and juries, and on film agents who are the creative factors in any deal.

As a lover, an active hand is quick to start. Foreplay lasts only a few moments, and then—"What are we waiting for?" With education, they can learn to allow a moment to linger and build momentum. This type can be romantic, especially if romance has an ingredient of challenge in it. They'll travel miles to see their lover.

They give good presents. They can be very attentive, but they can also be tiring. Their energy can exhaust you. Sometimes the active hand can be the most promiscuous of all hand types. Affairs or quick involvements can be the spice of life for their active appetites. An active's self-centeredness can be so overblown that he might think he deserves two lovers at the same time, regardless of whether he can handle two or not!

The competitive nature of actives can become a factor in love. They'll goad you into contests of who loves the most, who does the most for the other, or who expresses love most articulately. Time and mistakes, thankfully, usually teach the active hand to embrace the more constructive aspects of love.

♥ THE ANALYTICAL HAND ♥

The bony, narrow quality of the palm and defined knotty joints are the key aspects of *the analytical hand* (figure 7). The fingers are frequently on the long side, but the true distinguishing factor is the enlarged or knotty knuckles. The hand will often feel a little dry to the touch, sometimes cool.

Here is the personal computer who will put things in order, a complex and inventive individual who always reads between the lines to see what is really happening. These critics find joy in dissecting the poetry of John Donne, the stock market, or the ingredients of a mulligan stew. They get their kicks from analyzing things.

These individuals are restless and get bored easily unless they can keep their minds engaged in activity. This constant need to be thinking can be a blessing or a curse. It is very useful when it comes to making plans; all factors that are involved will be considered. On the down side, it can be difficult coping with one who is either always thinking or suffering from boredom when things are relaxed and easy.

These people have a tremendous appetite for variety, for lots of things that can be analyzed. Politics, art, economics, history, the neighborhood, the racial situation, our goals in space. They love the newspaper for its exciting array of facts and ideas, and they must read it every day. They savor trivia like chocolate. Any gathering

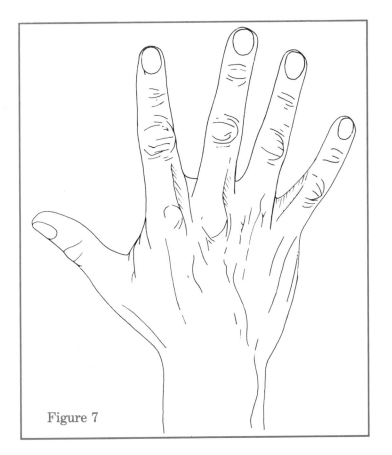

Figure 7

of information and its subsequent organization is of great importance to them. They make great writers, communicators, and consultants.

Being very socially aware and seeing beneath the surface of the social scene enables them to perceive the underlying motivations of humanity. Excellent in manners and protocol, career diplomats often have analytical hands.

Analyticals have an annoying habit of always being exactly on time; it's almost a hang-up with them. I have one client, an executive at a major movie studio, who has such a severe case of analytical hands that she's more than merely prompt—she's always early. Talk about organization—this woman actually alphabetizes her credit cards!

Inventive in the expression of facts and ideas, this hand type excels at presentation, legal argument, and philosophical debate. Though they are both efficient and utilitarian, many analytical individuals will complain that they feel disorganized (you can never be too thin, either).

Some have high mechanical aptitude and can repair anything. Surgeons are also found in this group, as are individuals who do extensive mathematical analysis or biological studies. Those who work with data and deal with the way that data goes from drawing board to actual objects and structures—from airplanes to sky-scrapers—are often of the analytical persuasion.

As lovers, men and women with analytical hands do best when love is on an installment plan, building it slowly and surely. Their very critical nature makes it difficult for them to get a relationship started. They overanalyze the moment, being either too romantic (depending on the heart line) or too cynical. They must examine every little thing—the smile, the looks, the words and the gestures, the places that you select to take them. These people can really put a situation under a microscope. They need to loosen up.

They are, however, very dependable. If the two of you agree to meet in Tangiers in two weeks at the Café Centrale, the analytical-handed partner will be there, at ten to two, waiting for you to appear. Their reliability and dependability is a strong recommendation.

Their analytical skills can also be useful to have on your side. They can build you up, point out all the good things you've got going for you, and see your deep inner talents. And then when they fight with you, of course, they will tell you of all the terrible traits you have and suggest that you catch up on some self-improvement.

Sexually this group can offer a wide spectrum of possibilities ranging from the normal old sex act to the analytically kinky. Usually, though, these are people who get into patterns of sexual behavior and do not break out of them, unless they have just read a book suggesting that they try something different.

One interesting consideration is that this type is great for sex when time is limited, since they understand that great things can happen in limited time slots and they have a built-in desire for everything to go off punctually.

You will find some members of this group advocating open or nontraditional relationships, but more often this is academic rhetoric which will not hold up in practice. In the final analysis, the analytical hand is more frequently monogamous and well grounded.

COMPARING HAND TYPES

Having looked at the four hand types, let's compare their romantic interactions. Each type of hand may be seen as an archetype representing a major personality type. The palm represents a major vibration, the bass note. Building on this bass note, the fingers and the Lines of Life, Head, and Heart contribute other vibrations that will be considered in later chapters. Then all factors blend together in the symphony of the whole person. For now, though, let's stick with the foundation upon which the rest of palmistry is built—the shapes of the hands.

After each of the following hand comparisons, you'll find a percentage number. This gives an approximate compatibility of the two hand types under consideration. The lowest number is 40 percent and the highest is 80 percent. The important thing to remember is that these percentages must be tallied with those percentages you'll find in comparing finger types and in the comparisons of the three major lines at the end of both of those chapters. Only the *total* of all five factors will have a significant meaning in accurate palmistry comparisons.

Realist and Realist:
Greatest strengths—same basic perceptions of the world; common ground in sensuality and earthiness; patient, common sense, materialistic, hardworking, dutiful, rational, objective goals, loyal, trusting, dedicated.

Greatest weaknesses—tolerance for repetition brings dullness or "The Great Rut"; sameness of common ground limits new growth; domineering nature of both makes for competition, stubbornness; overemphasis on materialism stunts potential emotional expression and growth.

♥   COMPATIBILITY: 80%

Realist and Receptive:

Greatest strengths—very different but complementary views of reality; the visionary and the realist. When roles are worked out, a very imaginative and resourceful blend; the realist gains sensitivity, the receptive gains groundedness.

Greatest weaknesses—two different emotional languages are spoken here; the receptive is often hurt or bored by the realist, while the realist is scornful of the receptive's soft-headedness. Good sex isn't everything.

♥   COMPATIBILITY: 40%

Realist and Analytical:

Greatest strengths—industrious, studious, methodical; passion builds from mental respect or mutual admiration; both are goal oriented, sensuous but not adventurous; very orderly, discriminating, practical.

Greatest weaknesses—critical, petty; both are self-indulgent and want the biggest piece of the love pie; greedy, jealous, competitive; pedantic versus practical.

♥   COMPATIBILITY: 75%

Realist and Active:

Greatest strengths—high motivation, realistic doers; passion finds a sensuous partner, kite finds a tail, patience meets impulse; plans become reality, dynamic direction with real results.

Greatest weaknesses—arguments over timing, in bed and out; stick-in-the-mud meets the prairie fire; realist's arrogance breeds intolerance; wobbling balance brings the active to eccentric behavior; both are competitive and often become argumentative.

♥   COMPATIBILITY: 60%

Receptive and Receptive:

Greatest strengths—very strongly intuitive, helpful, sympathetic, artistic, emotional, nurturing, tenacious, retentive; magnetic sex; sacrificing, musical, artistic; pools of passion.

Greatest weaknesses—very touchy, irritable, brooding; holding grudges, jealous, escapist tendencies, manipulative, hypochondriacal; sexually selfish, melancholy, moody, and misunderstood; highs and lows.

♥ COMPATIBILITY: 60%

Receptive and Analytical:

Greatest strengths—opposites attract, yin meets yang, psychic meets computer programmer, physics major dates New Age card reader; analytical is Sherlock Holmes in the sheets; receptive's insights are like a hypodermic needle that injects a feeling of love; irrational meets rational.

Greatest weaknesses—receptive thin-skinned, can pick fights over minor slights or because of mood; difference of reality perceptions make finding common ground difficult; suspicions overshadow trust; analytical can cut a dream with a knife, making sex juices run dry; receptive feels like a pin-cushion from analytical's mental jabs and complains of no physical passion; analytical wants to leave the airhead—opposites no longer attract.

♥ COMPATIBILITY: 45%

Receptive and Active:

Greatest strengths—intuition brings insight, radar guides the jet; sex is steamy and electric; fast-paced action, huge motivational leaps; great love-talk and all talk magnetic; where there is a will there is a way; generous, philosophical, enthusiastic, inventive, problem-solving.

Greatest weaknesses—active can experience burnout, infidelity, self-indulgence, impatience; receptive becomes sexually cold, taking impossible risks; tempers explode, exaggerated promises to renew fall short; both become vengeful, overbearing; active becomes pretentious as receptive broods and withdraws.

♥ COMPATIBILITY: 55%

Analytical and Analytical:

Greatest strengths—both very discriminating, subtle, exacting, clean, perfectionist, loyal, practical, thorough; willing to be patient for good sex; willing to study to improve love and sex; can follow directions, will spot flaws in dress or conduct before either is embarrassed by the gaff.

Greatest weaknesses—a debate society; both are never satisfied, closed-minded, inhibited, critical, snobbish, know-it-all; both have exclusive insights; mechanical sex, sadistic remarks; losing the forest for the trees.

♥ COMPATIBILITY: 70%

Analytical and Active:

Greatest strengths—active is like a rifle that finds in the analytical a telescopic sight; or the detective who finds a passion; philosophical conversation flows, sex is a work of art, bedroom talk is literate; their common motivation is goal-oriented; quick response time, courage of convictions, trained impulses; dexterous and talented, congenial.

Greatest weaknesses—active says go when analytical says no; mutual respect deteriorates to mutual competitiveness, making sex manipulative and without feeling; persuasiveness becomes prevarication and pretentiousness; active's optimism and motives are often questioned by analytical's need to show the reality of any issue.

♥ COMPATIBILITY: 70%

Active and Active:

Greatest strengths—energy to burn, to overwhelm; great expressive talents, lots of action, great at parties; torrid and passionate sex in various environments; strike when the iron is hot; social animals, romantic, giving, ambitious, broadminded, penetrating.

Greatest weaknesses—argumentative, temperamental, impatient; sex for sex's sake; self-centered, vain, cruel jokes; burning the candle at both ends means burnout; pretentious, autocratic, doing anything to win, morally ambivalent.

♥ COMPATIBILITY: 65%

MIXED HANDS AND FINGER PATTERNS

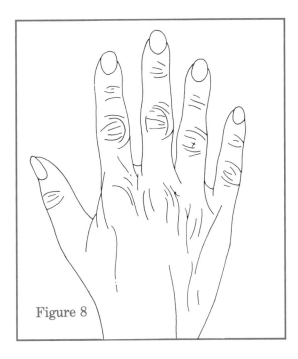

Figure 8

Imagine each of the four basic hand types to be a complete set—matching cups (fingers) and saucers (palm)—in four different patterns. The realistic palm—or saucer—has realistic fingers—or cup—and so on. In looking over your own hands, some of you may have noticed that your fingers and your palm are of seemingly different types. You may have smooth, meaty, or active palms with knotty, analytical fingers. If this is true, then you have a mixed hand—the palm and the fingers are of different types. This situation allows for certain dramatic changes in definition as hand characteristics blend. Even more complex and interesting is finding two or more different types of fingers on a palm—for example, receptive and analytical fingers on an active palm can be dynamite (figure 8). Let's look at the basic types of mixed hands and explain how to go about deciphering their unusual combinations of personality traits.

Use your own insights, based on the previous analysis of the basic hand types in relationships, to evaluate the romantic possibilities of such hand mixtures. You'll be able to assess what the individuals with these hand qualities might be like in relationships.

Realistic and Active Hand/Finger Mix—Powerful

The realist's ability to deal with the concrete is boosted by the energy of the active personality. This practical doer is highly motivated, a self-starter. This mix is good at sex, romantic enough, and a good provider. It is a strong, hard-working, and successful combination.

Active and Receptive Hand/Finger Mix—Magnetic

This type has a tendency to overindulge. The receptive personality has never met a buffet it didn't like, and the active thrust just serves to keep the appetite high. Love for this mix is as complex as *The Alexandria Quartet.* Lechery is possible, as is straight Madonna worship. Never boring, always developing new tastes, this mix is emotionally hot.

Realistic and Analytical Hand/Finger Mix—Judgmental

This judgmental person could spank you and then take you to bed. There is a need to be right all the time, to know it all—a frustrating need in this world of data explosion. In romance, this type "gives good gift" and wants good reward. Economically solid, the problem develops when success in the material world is viewed as grounds to be right in everything else. Ego is a problem here ("I make the money, I'll decide what's a good movie to see").

Realistic and Receptive Hand/Finger Mix—Productive

A great combination of intuition and groundedness; what more could you ask for? Don't ask. This mix is sensual, romantic, giving, inspiring. Weight gain is the only real problem that could make sex less than perfect. Everyone enjoys this person, as he is good with people.

Receptive and Analytical Hand/Finger Mix—Inventive

This mix will be very versatile in the bedroom. Little details will be attended to. Massage experts often have this blend. The receptive factor provides the intuition to know just where you itch, while the analytical part knows how to give the best scratch. These people have unusual personalities and interesting points of view.

When you are looking at a palm, remember that hand types are the most fundamental part of palmistry. But never forget that the human will may be the most powerful force of all. In your evaluations, look at all factors, as this overview will serve to make you a wiser, more accurate practitioner of this ancient and esteemed craft. As you are now an initiate of these honored mysteries, build your knowledge with the basics that I am teaching you, then cement your conclusions with the mortar of love and experience that is uniquely yours.

2

THE FINGERS and THUMBS

Imagine you are a parachutist, gliding to earth on wings of silk. The first things you see below you are lush green patches of color. Then, as your descent continues, the broad shapes of the forest become distinct, then the trees, then a particular tree, and suddenly a particular branch on the tree whose leaves are sticking into your face! You've landed. Metaphorically, this is how it is when learning to read and compare palms properly. First broad areas like hand types must be studied (the forest); then landmarks like the fingers and the thumb must be examined (the trees). We could carry this analogy to a comparison of the lines on the leaf to the lines on the hand, making the point that palmistry telescopes from the general to the particular.

In this chapter you will learn how the thumb and fingers give powerful, specific insights into understanding ourselves and our friends. We will spotlight a few important and easy-to-learn characteristics sifted from a large and ancient body of knowledge. Scholars like William G. Benham have written hundreds of pages about the fingers and thumb alone. And for good reason—the archetypal concepts of the hand types become more specifically focused personality traits through an examination of an individual's fingers and thumb. Some readers can even give a brilliant reading just by seeing the back of the hand and thumb. Once you've learned some of the ways to read the fingers and thumb, you'll be amazed at what you might observe watching television or film, as you catch a glimpse of a politician's hand or that of your favorite star.

We'll begin with the thumb. You may recall that medieval barons would hang their enemies by their thumbs. Were these old war lords onto something? Yes! Thumbs represent the human will, passion, and logic. To break the thumb is to break the will.

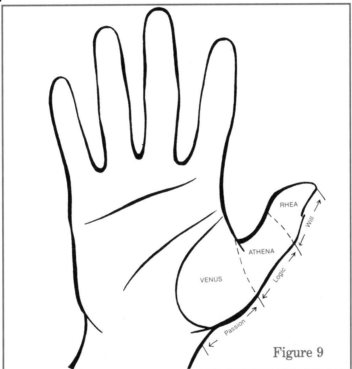

Figure 9

In examining the thumb (figure 9), you might find it helpful to know that its ruler is the goddess Rhea, the wife of Saturn. It was Rhea's will, instinct, and logic which enabled her to oppose her husband and save her children, the gods of Olympus. It seems fitting that the thumb, Rhea, opposes her husband Saturn (the middle finger), her son Jupiter (the index finger), and her grandsons Apollo (ring finger) and Mercury (little finger). This gives polarity to the hand, and provides a masculine and feminine balance. The base of the thumb is Venus, Rhea's granddaughter, the symbol of beauty and passion. The second phalange is Athena, also Rhea's granddaughter, and stands for cool logic, morality, and territoriality. We also see in Athena ethics and rationalism, as well as the sometimes illogical drive to make war. The tip of the thumb (the first phalange) is Rhea herself, the powerful instinctive will that can oppose the gods and be her own authority. If the thumb is strong, even the weakest hand can prevail. Rhea's power is in the alignment of human will with divine will. "Thy will be done" is the key. The individual with a strong thumb has a strong human will that aligns with Rhea, who adds her infinite will, her blessing to this person's drive for volution. This is the stuff that moves mountains. It is the stuff of a winner.

To evaluate the thumb, consider the following four aspects:

1 ♥ length
2 ♥ setting and stiffness
3 ♥ ratio of the three phalanges: the tip is will, the phalange is reason, the base is passion
4 ♥ the two visible joints: the upper joint is willfulness and the lower joint is timing. If there is a distinct knot or knuckle on the upper joint, there is an accentuated willpower; if such a knot shows on the lower joint, this indicates a well-developed sense of timing, as seen in the skills of a musician or a diplomat.

Traditionally, those with long thumbs have stronger willpower, whereas those with shorter thumbs are impulsive and need to hop around. Because willpower and stubbornness are linked, there are two thumb tests that indicate stubbornness: 1) if the thumb is inflexible, unable to make a ninety-degree angle with the index finger; or 2) if the third phalange (the tip) is longer than the second. Conversely, you can detect tact and sensitivity in the exercise of the will when you spot a "waisted" second phalange (the shape suggests an hourglass). This will hold true about 80 percent of the time.

In evaluating compatibility, know your own thumb first. Does it signal that you are a stubborn person? Then, compare yours to the thumb of the individual you are evaluating. The best match for someone with a strong thumb is someone with not quite as strong a thumb, because one of the two has to be more giving. The most difficult to deal with are those with weak thumbs. They can get emotionally messy and be flamboyant in making minor points. Two stubborn thumbs in combination can be difficult because their arguments last forever; yet when united for a common goal they can steamroll the opposition.

The setting of the thumb (figure 10) will tell you the instinctive nature of the thumb. The higher a thumb is placed in relation to the index finger, the more instinctive and primitive the emotions and the more quickly these emotions can change. Correspondingly, the lower the placement, the more logical and open to new ideas the instincts. Another characteristic manifested by thumb placement is versatility. The individual with a low-set thumb is good at many tasks, while the high-set thumb finds it harder to change routine. I have seen both types become C.E.O. of their companies, but they have very different managerial styles. The high-set thumb runs a tight ship, while the low-set thumb has a looser-running organization. The same is true in relationships: the high-set thumb looks for and demands the intense and traditionally defined relationship. Alternately, the low-set thumb tends to approach a relationship from a more experimental position.

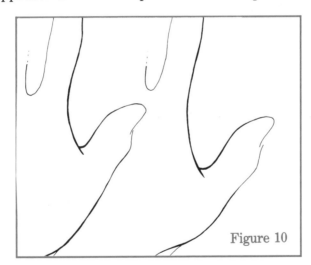

Figure 10

The Mount of Venus at the base of the thumb will tell a lot about a person's passions. A high, well-proportioned mount means that the individual is full of energy, is outgoing, has lots of interest in life, and can be very vital and enthusiastic. Those whose Mount of Venus is flat like a plateau are more mental in their energies. They like brainy pursuits, their friends are characters who resist the active mainstream of life, and their sense of discipline works best with specific mental activities like writers, sculptors, counterculture lawyers, community organizers, and rock climbers.

Since the Line of Life goes around the Mount of Venus, a favorable evaluation of this mount is very important. Individuals who have similar Mounts of Venus have less energy adjustment to make to one another; they are already tuned in to each other's basic life-force. If one has a high bulbous Venus and the other a flat plateau, then an adjustment has to be made between the raw biological energy of the one and the mental peculiarities of the other. This adjustment can be made, creating great, complementary relationships. But it takes work, and a lot of people will not work at a relationship.

The shape of the thumb's tip is a strong indicator of the inner power. A pointed or conic thumb is impulsive and quick to perceive, while a square thumb is a sign of common sense. A bulbous tip indicates a violent temper, and a tip that bends far back shows a far-out personality, usually artistic or involved in an exotic mental pursuit. A flat-tipped thumb is impatient and full of nervous energy; these are the expediters.

SIZING UP THE THUMB

When evaluating another person's thumb you should consider four main points: (1) length, (2) stiffness and setting, (3) ratio of the three phalanges, and (4) the type of Mount of Venus. Give each of these points on your own thumb a score of 10, for a total score of 40. Don't panic, this is a relative score. The idea is to see if another person's thumb is stronger by comparison. It's like the curve the teacher used to grade you with in high school. If someone scores a 35, they're under your thumb (sorry). If the thumb you're considering is stronger than yours and scores a 50, look out, this person is willful and could dominate you.

Let's break this process down. For each of the four qualities listed above, examine the target thumb and compare it to yours. Example: if your partner's thumb is longer than yours, give it a score of 11, 12, or 13, or more, depending on how much longer it is. Conversely, if the target thumb is shorter than yours, give it an 8 or less, depending on the shortness.

Repeat this comparative process with each aspect, remembering to use your thumb as a focal base point of 10 for each item. Thumb length is easily observable, as is the height or flatness of the Mount of Venus. The stiffness of the thumb can be casually felt or observed.

It takes some sophistication, though, to compute the ratios of Rhea and Athena to Venus. This means simply that the combined length of the first two phalanges of the thumb must be considered in relation to the length of bone under the fleshy part, Venus. Ideally the combination of Rhea and Venus will be slightly longer, meaning that will and reason can rule passion. Check out your thumb and give a 10 to whatever qualities you see there. Then compare the target thumb: Are Rhea and Athena longer or shorter than Venus? By how much, and how does this compare to yours?

Ideally it is good to actually measure these things, but this isn't always possible, so try to develop an eye for these comparisons.

	YOUR SCORE	LOVE INTEREST'S SCORE
THUMB LENGTH:	_____	_____
	____ 10	_____
SETTING/STIFFNESS:	_____	_____
	____ 10	_____
RATIO OF PHALANGES:	_____	_____
	____ 10	_____
MOUNT OF VENUS:	_____	_____
	____ 10	_____
TOTAL THUMB SCORE:	____ 40	_____

Finally, realize that this is an exercise in the observation of ratios: men usually have larger hands than women, and so it is the ratio of these proportions that counts. For example: suppose a woman has a large thumb for the size of her hand and the man she's observing has a small thumb for his hand. Even if that man's hand is physically larger, the woman should give him an 8 on thumb size because in actuality her thumb is stronger.

Remember, if a person's total score is over 40, his thumb is more powerful than yours. If it is less than 40, the thumb is not as powerful. Now ask yourself how you have performed in past relationships. Can you cope with a strong lover, or do you prefer to dominate? Keep this scoring method in mind and it will all come together when you evaluate the fingers. These scores will be used in the final compatibility scoring found at the end of Part One.

THE FINGERS

The four fingers are named for Roman gods. The index is Jupiter, the middle is Saturn, the ring is Apollo, and the little finger is Mercury. Each finger has a certain meaning based on its length, shape, and the ratio of its length to the others. Since the fingers function in a coordinated team effort, how they interrelate must be studied; yet each must be viewed as a single entity whose unique energies and specific traits influence the blend of the individual's personality.

MOUNTS

Mounts are pads of flesh at the base of each of the fingers. Pick up a hammer or a suitcase handle. It is the mounts that pad the base of the fingers, that get blistered. Sometimes they are a little off-center—a bit to the side of the base of each finger. I consider mounts to be a part of the fingers, and so I feel they should be studied as such. Only the Mounts of Mars negative, Luna, and Neptune exist without a joint to cover (see figure 1). Just as the Mount of Venus was studied as the base of the thumb (Rhea), the mounts at the base of each finger will be considered part of the corresponding finger. This serves to bring the mounts—too often studied separately—into the overall palmistry evaluation.

JUPITER: THE INDEX FINGER

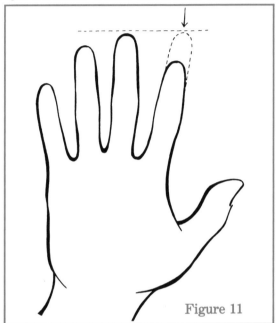

Figure 11

This is the finger of ambition, realistic perceptions, hunger for power, and great pride. Its importance and power cannot be overemphasized, as it gives a sense of authority, directedness, and candor. When it is normal in length, reaching the base of the nail of the middle finger, it represents the refined use of energy and direction, a leader with natural talent.

When the index finger is so long that it challenges the middle finger in length (figure 11), it can rightfully be called the Finger of Napoleon, for this person will likely be domineering and aggressively bossy—a little dictator. Those with this configuration have an exaggerated sense of self-importance; they can get things done, get the orders out, and delegate the assignments, but they can also provoke the troops to mutiny if they allow bossiness to prevail over flexibility. These individuals need to develop insights into themselves and accept their vulnerability honestly.

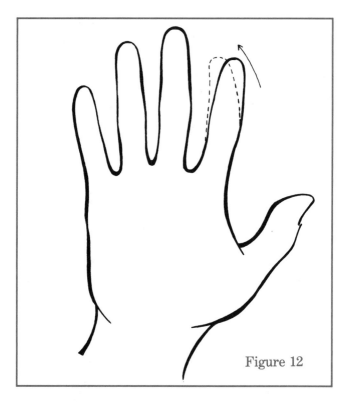

Figure 12

A short index finger limits leadership potential. Those with short index fingers tend to sidestep the limelight and the leadership role. They excel as sharp observers, and they are very good consultants who give wise—even bold—advice; yet they may also be impulsive and not very well grounded. Under pressure they may regress and become immature. As for relationships, they enjoy and function well with strong partners.

When the index finger curves toward the middle finger (figure 12), it means that the ego has been bent either by authority or circumstance. The individual with this curved finger is plagued with a sense of having to live up to some expectation, either that of a strong parent (who often possesses a strong religious or philosophical bent) or a very trying environment (tough economic or sociological conditions). He is a hard worker, but he can be restless, since his sense of self is dependent upon keeping active, constantly proving (and reproving) his self-worth. His ambition and drive can be quite strong, depending on finger length and mount height, but a curved index finger always indicates a need to prove oneself to an internal judge. Know that judge and you will understand the person.

The Mount of Jupiter at the base of the index finger indicates the level of resilience this individual has. If the mount is high and strong, the person has lots of ambition and takes a setback in stride. If the mount is flat—a plateau rather than an absence— the individual has a strong quality of mental aloofness; he is able to act coolly under pressure and keep a level head during critical times. Should the mount be lacking and the area flat, bony, or even concave, the person will not be resilient; he will actually suffer setbacks with difficulty. This individual lacks magnetism and needs a lot of time to rebuild confidence before hitting the path again.

The shape of the index finger gives us a clue as to the type of energy the individual possesses. (Refer back to the fingers in figure 3, the four basic hand types.) One with a square finger and slight knuckle is a practical person, a born leader. An active, smooth finger with a rounded tip shows a strong leader and a good speaker with artistic taste; this person is likely to be a restless soul. A person with a conic or receptive finger is very intuitive and artistic and can also be quite magnetic and sensitive. When very long, this type of index finger can signal aesthetic purity coupled with serious impracticality. Someone with an analytical finger and large knuckles is wonderful at research or leading groups that depend on highly compli- cated intellectual processes, but he tends to have difficulty with other types of groups, with common men looking for fast action. He lets attention to detail and correct process hang him up. With this type, a low-set thumb indicates greater flexibility and often signals a practical leader with an eye for detail.

Romantically speaking, the key to this Jupiter finger is the length. The longer the finger (figure 11) in relationship to the Finger of Saturn (the middle finger), the greater the tendency to dominate a lover by power or material means. These in- dividuals can overwhelm you. There is a certain bluntness in the long Finger of Jupiter, a feeling that might makes right. This translates into a good provider, but also a provider who says, "I make more money than you do, so we'll do it my way." The very long Jupiter looks upon a lover as a reward won. And if they've won you, they own you.

The medium-length Jupiter finger (ending near the nail) is a sign of self-confidence, consideration, and willingness to see the other (that is, your) side of a situation. These people have the decisiveness to make a commitment without the need to dominate.

The short Jupiter finger (ending near the first joint of the Finger of Saturn) is the reverse of the long—it signals a wimp. These people will revel in giving up their decision-making ability to you. They will need to be pumped up with praise to gain self-confidence, although they do possess great loyalty and will stick to a relationship even if their partner gets sick or is gone for long periods of time. In short, this type is the enlisted soldier in the army of love. If you like a yes person to snuggle up to, here is your ticket.

SATURN: THE MIDDLE FINGER

Saturn is traditionally seen as a stern god, a god of judgment and limitation. The middle finger is the fulcrum of the hand and its symbolism centers around the superego, the conscience, and the lasting, eternal concepts that imbue existence with metaphysical meaning—in essence, the values that balance the personality. Saturn should be the longest finger in the hand; if not, another energy has replaced it as the most powerful, and this is not desirable. Individuals with longer Jupiters or Apollos are psychologically lopsided. They take extreme positions and lack balance. They are usually emotionally compulsive and self-seeking in the extreme, often attracting masochistic types as partners.

Conversely, an overly long middle finger that extends greatly beyond the ring and index fingers represents someone whose conscience is very strong, whose ability to savor life is dependent upon his living up to special standards and codes—religious, spiritual, or ethical. This person often views experience through the filter of moral allegory and sees life as hard work and sacrifice.

A challenge to the length of the middle finger by both adjoining fingers (figure 13) is a sign of restlessness. Because the fulcrum of the middle finger is challenged, the person swings from one polarity to another and can't enjoy true peace of mind. These individuals are always striving, convinced that "if only I could get such-and-such, I could be happy." Then when they get "such-and-such," their thoughts turn to other things and once again joy eludes them. They will never find a happiness they can enjoy and savor as much as the quest, the striving. Put simply, theirs is a case of "the grass is always greener on the other side of the fence." This person might quip, with Groucho Marx, "I'd never join a club that would let me in."

A middle finger that is at least a fingernail longer than either of the adjoining fingers symbolizes a good balance. Individuals with this configuration can enjoy themselves, attain real peace of mind, and keep their acts together. They have no particular ax to grind, and can respond honestly in relationships.

When the Apollo and Jupiter fingers are of equal length, close to the base of the nail of Saturn (figure 14), you have a diplomat. These people can move among idealists and realists, liberal and conservative, rich and poor, with the same openness and equanimity. Their versatility makes them good partners.

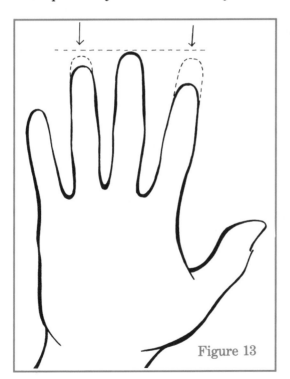

Figure 13

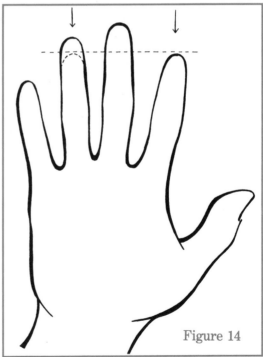

Figure 14

It is a dangerous sign when the middle finger leans toward the index finger; it indicates that the ego is stronger than the underlying moral values of the person and that he may therefore consider himself at times to be above the law. A print of Hitler's hand reveals this configuration. Consider carefully this individual whose ego is a court of law unto itself. You may have to work for an egomaniac like this, but you'd sure like to avoid dating one. Remember, people are often on best behavior when you first meet them, but the fingers speak the truth right away.

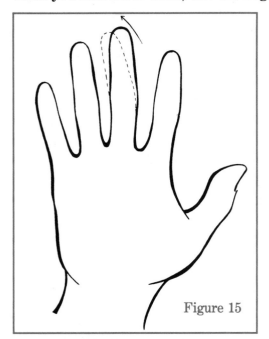

Figure 15

The middle finger leaning toward the ring finger (figure 15) is a sign of an individual who is good at planning and can deal with diplomatic structures and red tape. These people are also often didactic about art being the true God. For them, art is the true expression of the human will; therefore art is divine, for the human will is a microcosm of the divine will. When the ring finger curves toward the middle finger, there exists the same good planning, but this individual sees art as a didactic form—it must always express a specific point of view. Individuals whose fingers curve this way will have definite ideas about what God or some other power meant art to be and the ideas it should express. Art, for them, must reveal that there is a moral force in the universe. Limiting though this concept may be, many people still believe in such morality, and their arguments can be persuasive.

The realistic or square-tipped middle finger indicates a practical, pragmatic vision of values and philosophy. The smooth, firm, round-tipped active finger belongs to an explorer of values, one who always wants to see how values work in real life. The conic, receptive middle finger reveals a very tuned-in person who seeks a unique, higher code. This search can sometimes settle on an intense traditional religious concept or indicate a mystical, psychic nature. The analytical, knotty-jointed middle finger is that of the philosopher looking at the reasons why things are the way they are. This individual will study many ways of thinking and believing before settling on a belief of his own.

The Mount of Saturn at the base of the middle finger gives a clue to the fullness of a person's conscience and resolve. A well-developed, rounded mount indicates that the person has a good practical philosophy of life, but is able to forgive and forget, to adjust to life as it comes. A flat, plateau mount under Saturn indicates a tough, iron resolve. These people dig in and are self-disciplined—maybe too much so. They can often espouse the belief "If I did it this way, so can you." It is harder for them to forgive than it is for others. Finally, if there is no mount under Saturn, these individuals can be swayed this way and that, for they lack real moral fiber and don't persevere as hard as they should. Direct these individuals to the self-help rack of your local book store.

Romantically speaking, the key to the Finger of Saturn is its length and straightness. The crooked or bent finger will have a didactic attitude that is not as interested in romance as it is in dogma. This individual will extol the virtues of romance, but pout for days if you make him change his plans, or didn't just love the movie he loved, or failed to vote the way he voted. Moral conformity enters into romance with Saturn's crooked finger. If your Saturn is crooked too, and your morals align, it's a match made by Saturn.

The long Finger of Saturn has the advantage of great commitment and balance. It can ground a love in the fertile earth of honest work and the willingness to till the soil. These individuals do not change their affections easily. This is Penelope at the loom.

The short Saturn means commitments can change more rapidly. This person's loyalty to a loved one may not be as strong as his loyalty to an ambition. As a wife or girlfriend, husband or boyfriend, you must fit into the changing environment occasioned by the climb to the top. Become a liability at the next circle of parties and you'll be dropped like a bad stock. The short Saturn does enjoy the advantage of being more adventuresome than his longer sibling, so if you can handle the fast lane, this could be it.

APOLLO: THE RING FINGER

Apollo, for whom the ring finger is named, is the Greek god who pulled the sun around the heavens behind his golden chariot. He is also the god of the healing arts, aesthetics, music, physical beauty, and grace. Apollo claimed he would never marry, but he did, so it is a fitting irony that it is around his namesake fingers that the wedding band is placed.

The ring finger represents our attitudes toward style, diplomacy, class (as in classy taste), motivation. The key is in realizing that the length and shape of the Finger of Apollo will reveal how these elements are manifesting in an individual.

When the ring finger is as big as the middle of the nail of Saturn (figure 16A), you have someone who is able to seduce almost anyone. Some authorities call a long ring finger the sign of the gambler. My "hands-on" experience, which I acquired reading palms at a Kentucky Derby party, proved to me that this is inaccurate. There were an equal number of long Jupiters and long Apollos among the gambling crowd there, as well as in other venues where I've done readings for avowed lovers of gambling. What a long Apollo *does* signal is a person who wants to lead by motivation, the grand idea, and clever design. This individual puts a carrot in front of the horse and uses personal magnetism instead of power or authority to get people going. This is in distinct contrast to the power-pushing long Finger of Jupiter, who motivates with the proverbial big stick.

A normal ring finger reaches the bottom of the fingernail of the middle finger (figure 16B). This individual has a balanced approach to art, style, personal direction, and motivation. They dress well, but don't bowl you over with their "I just stepped out of a fashion magazine" appearance. They are excellent diplomats and can work skillfully in tight situations. In personal relationships, they work hard on the give and take of the interaction. They can be very creative and their powers of perception are quite strong.

When the ring finger is short (figure 16C), not reaching to the base of the nail on Saturn, there is an imitative quality in the creativity of the individual. These individuals like commercial art, and may select designer materials that gloss over their individuality. They don't possess the flair to be expansive with the imagination.

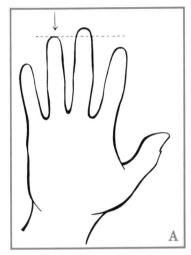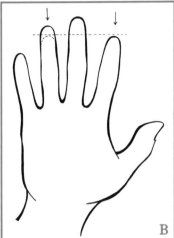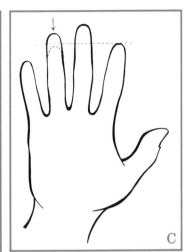

Figure 16

Here is the technician whose creativity is in knowing the logic of electrical cords and lighting, of dye processes, of software disks. Look for a strong thumb or Jupiter to contribute the power that brings success.

The Mount of Apollo at the foot of the ring finger indicates the energy needed to express the creative talents of the individual with honesty and enthusiasm. A large, well-developed mount indicates a person who has a lot of energy for expression, who feels the joie de vivre very deeply and is magnetic and charming. The plateau-shaped mount indicates a strong interest in mental expression, in the way form shapes content, in the way style and cut make color work in different ways. These people can be snobs about taste. A weak or underdeveloped Mount of Apollo indicates an imitative style; these people are "knock-off specialists," feeding on the creativity of others. They can make a fortune delivering something similar to and cheaper than the original. They copy their friends' dress or style. When the finger is normal or long with this weak mount the individual excels in crafts, where symmetry is important.

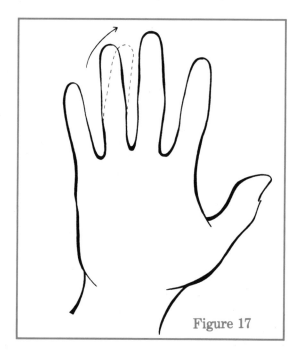

Figure 17

When the Finger of Apollo curves toward Saturn (figure 17), it is an indication that the person can organize well but is didactic in outlook. Planning takes precedence over spontaneity. These folks don't like surprises. Alternatively, when Apollo curves toward Mercury, you have a person who has made a great art out of talking, so great that he sometimes sacrifices reality and truth for the sake of a good story or presentation. Remember not to believe all you hear!

Romantically, the Finger of Apollo must be longer than the first joint of the Finger of Saturn. When the finger is this long or longer, there is ample aesthetic sensitivity in the individual to enhance a relationship. Spontaneous feelings, appreciation of the nuances of life, the ability to shape an uplifting opinion about love, to plan romantic moments, all these are within the realm of Apollo.

Apollo was a healer, and a short (figure 16C) Apollo indicates an individual who lacks the ability to get over a fight or disagreement readily, to forgive. A longer

Apollo is capable not only of forgiving, but also of being sorry. The short Apollo is more childish, and a child always thinks that what it wants is right.

A person who has an Apollo that bends toward Saturn has a single romantic concept in his mind, which he worships like a deity. Betray this concept—his idea of the perfect girlfriend, the perfect wife, the perfect mother or hostess—and you have betrayed a religious truth, for which you will face the fury of hell. However, if the two of you agree on this romantic concept, you may have a mate for life.

Should Apollo bend toward the Finger of Mercury, take a pass on the relationship. Why? Because there will be more promises than reality in the love given. This is a rare way for Apollo to bend, but when it does you can bet that there is a lot of wind and not much action—such a partner will promise you anything and give you nothing.

Apollo is the finger of possibilities. If Jupiter is the finger of the realist, the no-nonsense person, then Apollo is the finger of the idealist, the one who is motivated by the beauty of an idea or by taking a chance. A finely shaped Apollo is a sure sign of a sensitive lover, someone who can share in feelings and appreciate the tenderness of a moment. It is common in the hands of artists and businessmen who make an art of their work. Always evaluate this finger with special care, for Apollo can light the lamp of love in the most beautiful and rewarding ways.

MERCURY: THE LITTLE FINGER

It is fitting that the Finger of Mercury is next to Apollo. When Mercury was born, he immediately stole two of Apollo's favorite cows, feasted on them, invented the lyre from their remains, and then talked Jupiter and Apollo into accepting him as the twelfth and youngest of the great gods of Olympus.

Mercury is the god of communication, divination, businessmen, and thieves. He delivers all the messages for the gods. Fleet of foot, he always knows what is happening. Thus, the little finger represents the networking center of the individual. Though small in size, this finger is mighty in meaning. Its dimensions indicate how well a person can communicate, how honest he tends to be, how much he can twist language to make a point, how well he keeps secrets.

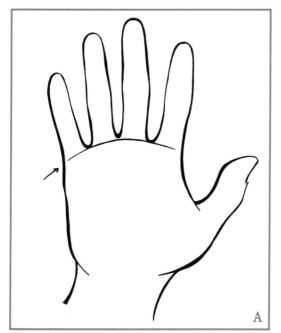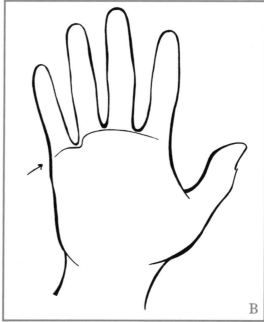

Figure 18

First look to see if the finger is set evenly at the base with the Finger of Apollo (figure 18A). If the bases are even, the finger is normal; if Mercury is set lower (a quarter inch), as if on a lower step (figure 18B), it is a sign of potentially low self-esteem. The low-set finger often indicates a late bloomer, someone who comes into his own glory farther down the road than someone with a normally set finger.

Looking at Mercury, compare its length to the flexure line at the first joint (the point of mental organization) of the Finger of Apollo (figure 19). If the little finger reaches above the first joint (A) of the ring finger, the person is a boundless talker, a storyteller who can yak your ears off. These people are excellent in marketing, especially telemarketing. Of course, in romance they have a "line" that is as long as your arm. They are the life of the party and know lots of gossip, but don't believe everything they tell you.

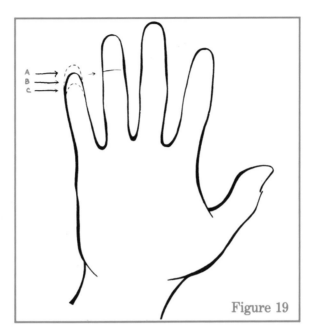

Figure 19

If the little finger is even with the first joint on Apollo (19B), these individuals are very honest and forthright in communication. They are good at honest evaluation. Being sharp, objective observers, they can give clear professional opinions. They will not overpraise you (as the long Mercury will); they say only what they really think.

If the little finger does not reach the first joint of Apollo (19C), the individual is understated. These people don't like to talk if they can't say something positive. Sometimes shy, they may not like to say a lot even if they know a lot. They must be drawn out from their shell and made to feel at ease. These individuals are the most masterful observers. They have a lot to offer, but getting them to share these insights, getting them to articulate their feelings, can be a challenge. These people are often clever at saying something simple and vague to throw you off track. For example, if you ask them what they did on a date or an outing, they will reply with "Oh, the usual," or "visited a lot of places." When you probe deeper you will find they did a lot more than that!

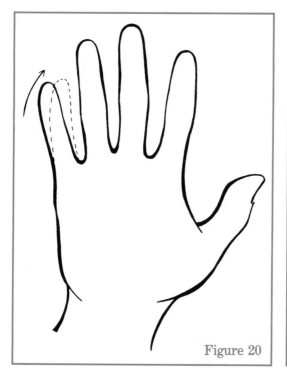

Figure 20

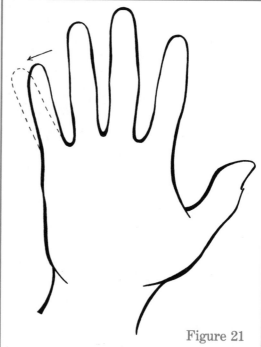

Figure 21

The receptive, pointed little finger as shown in the basic hand-shape types (figure 20) indicates someone who is very insightful about what makes others tick and can express these pearls of wisdom in the form of real zingers. Someone with the realistic, square-tipped little finger is a practical speaker who likes to use old bromides everyone understands. In contrast, one with the smooth, round-tipped, active little finger is restless and very energetic in making a point; and finally, an individual with the analytical little finger and developed knuckles is a very orderly, precise communicator with a predilection for written language and the ability to be very concise—even laconic—in speech.

When the little finger curves toward the Finger of Apollo (figure 20), the person can keep secrets very well and is a master talker, able to sell the sizzle. This person can fall in love with his own voice and stretch the truth to fit any desired purpose.

There is a bit of the defense lawyer to this formation, for he likes to debate both sides of an issue, just for fun.

When the little finger leans away from the finger of Apollo (figure 21), the individual is a maverick who goes his own way and follows his own drummer. These people will not hesitate in seeking their own path when the way of the crowd becomes too much of a compromise. In romance they will be headstrong, willing to go to great lengths to protect their individuality, to do it their way.

Romantically, the Finger of Mercury should be considered the key to how an individual will communicate, and to the pace he or she may want to pursue in a relationship. The longer the finger, the more talkative the person will be. Outrageous claims of affection are likely. However, this is counterbalanced by the fact that those with long fingers are often the life of the party, and can generate a good time wherever they are.

Those with a medium-length Mercury are the honest ones, who will be supportive and helpful, and will not stretch their statements to meet their imagination. These are solid individuals in a relationship.

Short little fingers are secretive, they will not tell on you, and they are more likely to get you to tell them your secrets. These individuals are masters of understatement. "Where did you go?" "Drive-in movie." "Did you like it?" "What I saw." In love, too, they have the knack of making a little say a lot.

RATIOS AND RELATIONSHIPS

Einstein taught that everything is relative, and this is especially true in palmistry. The *ratios of the length of the fingers to the palm* and the *ratio of the length of the fingers to one another* reveal some very powerful energies of the individual's personality. When studying the bones of the hand, you are studying the primitive claw structure modernized by gradual evolution. Fingers that might look long may really be considered short—if the palm to which they are attached is a lot longer. Ideally, fingers should be the same length as the palm (within three-eighths of an inch) for the individual to be considered as having a totally balanced personality. Try to develop an eye for making this survey of ratios in an instant.

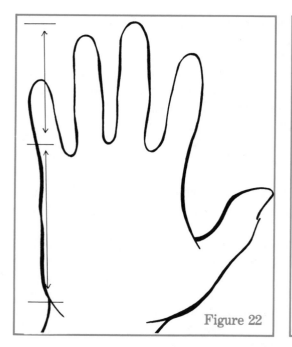

Figure 22

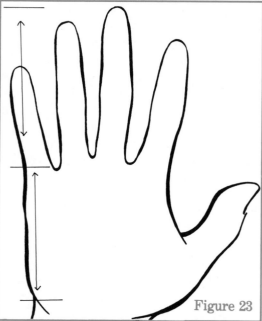

Figure 23

Those with balanced palm and finger lengths have an ideal combination. They are able to work quickly and thoroughly, with both an eye for detail and the gift of expedition. I have seen pilots, executives, skilled physicians, world-class photographers, and other gifted individuals with this hand. As lovers they are versatile and able to share in a large variety of activities. They possess an emotional balance that allows them to be even-tempered and socially skilled.

Those with fingers that are shorter than the palm (figure 22) are quick and impulsive. They chafe under detail work, preferring to expend energy meeting people and keeping things moving. They make good executives if they have detail-oriented individuals to take care of the paper work they generate. I am reminded of one executive I met who had short fingers. When I asked him about how he made deals, he told me, "I make the deal and then I tell my lawyer to write the law around it." Always impatient, they are spontaneous lovers, and will want to see the action move along. They hate to wait for anything, so they are good when schedules are tight. They love the adrenaline rush of a romance on the run.

Those with fingers that are longer than the palm (figure 23) are perfectionists who take their time at whatever they do. They will send the food back in restaurants and give a long analysis of the movie they've just seen. As lovers they are patient, wanting to establish a solid base to build upon. Sometimes with them it will seem like things are going a little slowly, but with steady developments; like a fine wine in the cellar, things will get better and better. This type will be philosophical, wanting to dig into something more deeply than is necessary to get the job done. Usually those with long fingers give great back rubs, whereas those with short fingers give quickies and "tire" easily.

Finger lengths are a real clue to the rhythms of an individual. A handy metaphor to remember this by is shown in the simple "wave theory": short fingers are short waves, moving quickly with high frequency. The longer the fingers, the longer the "wavelength" and thus the lower the frequency. In love, having the right vibra-tions between two people is most important, and the fingers can supply a great deal of insight as to whether the matching "vibes" are there. If you like to tune in to impulsive and very active types, look for short fingers. If you like a slower pace, a more philosophical approach, consider someone with long fingers.

The ratio of the length of the Finger of Jupiter to that of Apollo can also give you important clues to a person's mental outlook. When Jupiter is longer than Apollo (figure 24A), the individual is realistic, aggressive, and a little bossy. A person who motivates with direct pushing, Jupiter people are good at confrontation, mediation, head-on negotiation, and objective evaluations.

When the finger of Apollo is longer than that of Jupiter (figure 24B) the individual

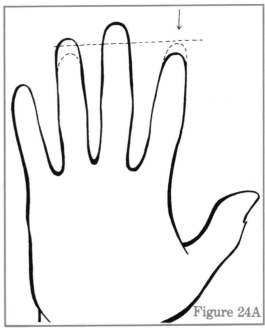

Figure 24A

will have an idealistic approach to things. Motivation is indirect, invoking the need to aspire to high ideals to reach the best in oneself, to do it with style, to have class. The Apollo individual is subtle, often more interested in the way things are done than in the compensation for doing them. They are masters of getting a consensus and do not like raw confrontation. They also seem to always be drawn into office intrigues that end with someone's resignation. They have no interest in being hatchet men, but will not blanch at the task if they must undertake it. They are romantic and are willing to take risks; they have an intuitive side and are discreet. Jupiter is more realistic, Apollo more idealistic. Take your pick. Some like their romance straight; others like theirs on ice.

Also note how the hand is held naturally. If there is a wide space between Jupiter and Saturn (dotted line, figure 25A), the person is open-minded. If Jupiter and Saturn are really close together (solid lines), the person is conservative. If the Finger of Mercury is held near Apollo (figure 25B), the individual will want to undertake a conservative or middle-of-the-road approach to his activities. If there is a wide space between Mercury and Apollo (25B, the dotted line), the person is a maverick despite the Jupiter-Saturn position.

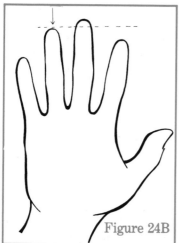

Figure 24B

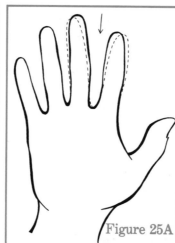

Figure 25A

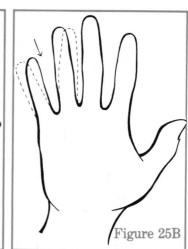

Figure 25B

An example of how to read this: If a person has a tight Jupiter-to-Saturn and a wide Mercury-to-Apollo, he may act uptight, but when the time is right, he'll get down and party. These individuals might be termed "all do and no say." The reverse, a wide space between Jupiter and Saturn with Mercury close to Apollo, symbolizes the "all think and no do" person. Example: He will sign a petition for a nude beach because he believes in the right for a nude beach. Yet he won't take his clothes off when he goes there. Or she may be for abortion yet wouldn't get one herself.

PUTTING IT TOGETHER

The following method of compatibility evaluation is based on a method similar to one I learned at Toastmasters for evaluating speeches. The first speaker is given a score of 10, and then every speaker who follows is judged against that base score. If the second speaker is not as good, he will receive a score of 7 or 6, depending on his skills relative to the first speaker. Each speech is then scored in like manner— comparing it to the first speaker and scoring it relative to the score of 10. If a speaker comes to the podium and far surpasses the first speaker, he will receive a score of 12 or 13, and so on.

When evaluating the significance of the fingers in regard to compatibility, think of yourself as the first speaker and assign each finger a base score of 10. At the same time, take into careful consideration the qualities of your hand; these are the qualities to which you will be comparing and scoring your love interest's qualities.

1 ♥ Are your fingers short and quick or long and deliberate?
2 ♥ Is Jupiter or Apollo dominant?
3 ♥ Are any of your fingers bent? If so, what quality does this give you?
4 ♥ Consider the shape and meaning of the fingers in the four major hand types: active, receptive, analytical, and realistic.

Put this all together. It's a little like evaluating a small laundry list of your important features. Below is a sample scoring sheet that I've filled out with my own answers to the four questions above. Follow it as you fill out the blank sample at the end of this explanation. I have the short, quick fingers (impulsive), the dominant Apollo (idealistic), a bent or curved Saturn (verbal, didactic), and my hand type is strongly active. Again, because my hand is the reference point, I score each of the four with a 10, giving me a total score of 40. So will you.

Then you will view the hand of the individual in question and quickly evaluate it, taking note of the salient characteristics. Let's take another laundry list and compare it to my list evaluated at 40 for the thumb score that I explained earlier, and now 40 for the fingers. This young woman that I am considering has long fingers (deliberate), and compared to mine they will earn a higher score—a 15. She has a dominant Jupiter (double realistic) and thus earns a higher score here as well—15. Her Mercury is short and curved (a talker), without conflict to my verbal nature. This is scored as a 10. Finally, the overall shape of her fingers belongs to the realistic (strong) hand type and this balances with mine, which is active/receptive, giving her another score of 10 for this feature. Her total score, then, is 50.

In sum, I've judged that this lady's finger structure is 10 points or 20 percent stronger than mine (she'll be picky and bossy, and that bothers me), on the basis of the Jupiter-to-Apollo comparison and her long-fingered, perfectionist's traits, which may well slow me down. Our thumb scores, which I figured separately, were balanced, giving us each a score of 40. Thus, the totals (fingers and thumb) are 80 for me and 90 for this realistic woman. This is going to be a stretch: she would probably be a great friend or working pal. But I would probably find her either demanding or boring as a lover. It's possible that with all her Jupiter dominance she might just try to take me over. But this isn't likely. I know what works for me; if I were smart, I would pass. Use this method and discover what works for you. Look at the list and keep your mind open.

Remember, the fingers and thumb speak very clearly if you listen and take the time to evaluate them in this manner. However, don't draw any hasty conclusions until you have examined the stories told in the Lines of Life, Heart, and Head. And save the calculations that you made in this section to use in the final tabulation of compatibility at the end of Part One.

	YOUR SCORE	LOVE INTEREST'S SCORE
FINGER LENGTH:	_ short, quick _____	long, deliberate _____
	____ 10 _____	15 _____
FINGER DOMINANT:	_ Apollo—idealist _____	Jupiter—realist _____
	____ 10 _____	15 _____
BENT FINGERS:	_ Saturn—didactic _____	Mercury—debator ____
	____ 10 _____	10 _____
BASIC TYPE:	_ Active _____	Realistic _____
	____ 10 _____	10 _____
THUMB SCORES:	____ 40 _____	40 _____
TOTAL:	____ 80 _____	90 _____

SAMPLE SCORE SHEET

	YOUR SCORE	LOVE INTEREST'S SCORE
FINGER LENGTH:	_____	_____
	____ 10 _____	
FINGER DOMINANT:	_____	_____
	____ 10 _____	
BENT FINGERS:	_____	_____
	____ 10 _____	
BASIC TYPE:	_____	_____
	____ 10 _____	
THUMB:	____ 40 _____	
TOTAL:	____ 80 _____	

3

THE LINE of LIFE

No other aspect of palmistry has the mystery and the romance of the Line of Life (figure 26A). Here is a line surely like the very thread of life woven by one of the goddesses of Fate, Clotho. According to mythology, Clotho spins this vital thread, her sister Lachesis measures its length and indicates how long the individual will live, and the third sister of Fate, Atropos, cuts the thread that ends the life. This symbolism is often projected onto the Line of Life.

The first question a palmist often hears is "How long is my Life Line?" The myth endures in the face of modern science and human heart transplants that somehow we can gauge the length of life by a line on the palm. If this were true, how much easier it would be to plan our lives, to know which planes to take, and how to save or spend our money ("Baby, we're at the end of our Life Lines, let's spend our nest egg").

The Line of Life is not meant to reveal when one dies but to describe the way one lives. This is the key to understanding this majestic and wonderfully symbolic river of the life-force. As it flows, so flows the elixir, that mysterious energy that inhabits us, animates us, and is destined to leave us. In a true sense, the Life Line is the record of the soul's journey through time and flesh.

The Line of Life originates on the thumb side between the Mounts of Jupiter and Mars, symbolizing that we are born out of ambition (Jupiter) and fiery passion (Mars).

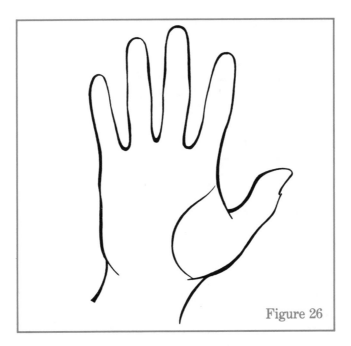

Figure 26

This line curves around the base of the thumb, dividing the Mount of Venus from the Plain of Mars, the flat of the palm, the way the Rio Grande separates the United States and Mexico. The line can be visualized as a dynamic tightrope between Venus (beauty and passion) and Mars (aggression and vigor). Any breaks in the line, any changes in course, all reflect a change in the dynamics. Does Venus pull the line in tight to the thumb and make a homebody of Mars, or does Mars pull the line out on the plain and make Venus do a jitterbug?

Seeing the symbolism and personally interpreting a line without referring to this or any other book is the heart of learning palmistry. Know the map of the hand and the myths of the symbolic rulers of gods, and you have the basic tools. When you have a live hand in front of you, you can't excuse yourself and go to the books! In this palm you will have to read what you can make of the symbolism and what your intuition tells you. With practice, you'll be able to read the real person with confidence. The lines will speak to you, telling you their secrets.

THE NATURE OF THE LINE

The quality of a line is of the greatest importance. Quality is evaluated by the depth and the texture of the line—the latter indicative of complications in the flow. Think of the line as a river of life. You need to consider how deep and wide it is. Let's look at this in detail.

There are three basic variations in the depth of the Line of Life, each with a distinct meaning: deep, normal, and shallow. Those with a deep line have the vigor of a locomotive high-balling through the Midwest. Their energy is boundless; they are able to do lots of work and they can be athletic, or they can take this energy and eat until they're very fat. Still, the energy is overwhelming. They keep up a constant barrage of patter, talking, and pushing. They can be a formidable opponent when pitted against you, or a great ally when on your side. When this quality of line is present, it gives whatever patterns that exist on the hand a very strong charge of biological power. Think of this line as the deep river of life through which the gusty emotions flow with great power.

The average or normal Line of Life is well marked and well delineated, but not as overwhelming as the deep Line of Life. An average line indicates that the individual is balanced. It is deep enough to be a furrow, but not deep enough to be a ravine. These people are able to work hard and play hard, but they can also rest and take breaks without having always to be on the go. These individuals have good health and good athletic ability, and they are solid workers. They can hold their own.

The great strength of individuals with a shallow Line of Life is the tremendous sensitivity they bring to any endeavor. These people are human seismographs. Their difficulty is that they do not have as much energy and drive as those with deeper Life Lines. Therefore, these people can be overwhelmed by the energy of another person and end up doing things they don't want to do, and wind up with headaches and all sorts of real or imagined ailments. Those with shallow lines must learn to develop their willpower and keep themselves away from magnetic individuals, especially those whose energy excites them for a while but eventually proves a source of domination and potential harassment.

DEVIATIONS IN THE LIFE LINE

Any change in the line from a clear smooth crease has meaning. Lines that shoot off up toward the fingers (figure 26B) represent an effort to achieve a goal, one that may be indicated by the finger to which the line points. Jupiter means ambition, Saturn stability, Apollo art, and Mercury communication. If the branch shoots out into the Plain of Mars it indicates travel or some type of exploration.

Lines that cross the Line of Life are called *interference lines* (figure 27). Usually these lines come from the Mount of Venus and indicate that a family member or another loved one is trying to influence your life. It is hard to pinpoint what, exactly, this influence might be, but the closer the interference lines are to the start of the line on Mars positive, the more likely the parents are involved.

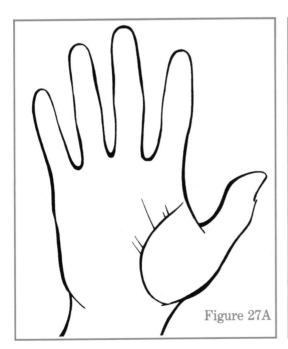

Figure 27A

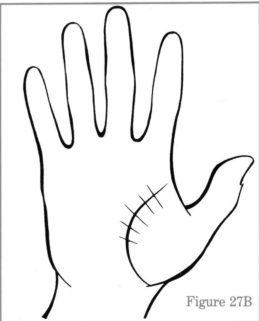

Figure 27B

The intensity of the interference is represented by the number and depth of the lines crossing the Life Line. The wider and deeper the lines that form the intersection, the larger the possible crisis. Deep interference lines are a signal that outside forces are seeking to block your chosen path. A series of light interference lines represents more of a nagging, continuing irritation to the energy of the life flow, not the crisis-invoking challenge of the heavy lines. If you are considering matrimony with a person with lots of deep interference lines, usually you're marrying the whole family and possibly a whole lot of trouble. Maybe you need that; maybe you don't.

Figure 28

Any islanding, fraying, or feathering (figure 28) of the Life Line indicates that the life-force will be diminished in energy, diffused or split in some way by a complex situation. These deviations always mean that complete efforts are difficult, since the individual's energy is not at full force. Some old palmistry books warn of illness arising out of these configurations, but the trouble may actually be psychological or emotional.

To tell age on the Line of Life, consider how you measure mileage on a road map. Figure the beginning of the Life Line is day one and all the way around to the edge of where the thumb meets the wrist is age ninety (figure 29). Midway between those two points is forty-five, and so on. But don't get hung up on this method of age and time measurement. It's not as accurate as it is claimed to be. Remember that one's will also plays a part in one's fate, and a positive attitude can make conflicts an opportunity. The depth of the lines is really your best measuring stick for vitality judgments.

THE INNER LINE OF LIFE

On some hands a sister line, the Inner Line of Life, can be seen running inside the Line of Life, closer to the thumb. This line gives strength in resisting interference lines and symbolizes extra physical vitality and strong inner character. Sometimes

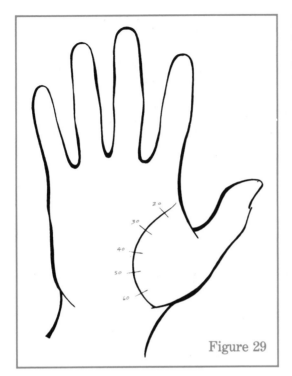

Figure 29

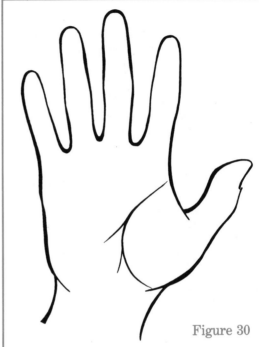

Figure 30

termed "the inner empathy line" by older palmists, it helps hold life together and deepens spiritual sensitivity.

TRAVEL FORK

A fork at the end of, or branching from, the Life Line is considered a travel line (figure 30). A large branch from the Life Line out toward the Luna/Neptune edge of the palm is also considered a travel line. Look for these forks and branches as a sign that the life-force likes to wander a bit. And remember, the longer the fork, the bigger the itchy foot.

PATTERNS

The larger patterns of the Lines of Life are very important. In this section I have condensed a great deal of information into models for comparison. When considering the following patterns, realize that these are large frames with which to organize and compare. Consider them like the constellations—there are lots of different ways of seeing a configuration, but what's important is finding the key points of light, the matrix of the pattern.

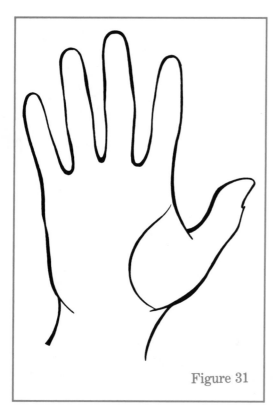

Figure 31

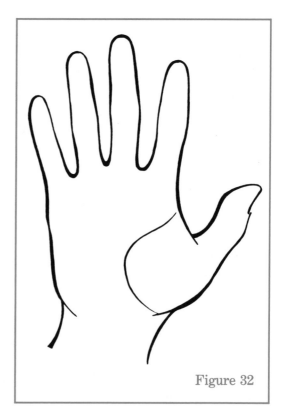

Figure 32

THE CLOSE LINE OF LIFE: HOME SWEET HOME

This Line of Life stays very close to the thumb (figure 31), tightly circling the Mount of Venus. These people like the place where they were born and don't stray far from it. They have roots that are deep. These individuals usually know a lot about their native region and have a few stories extolling its virtues. They take pride in odd little titles that the chamber of commerce has dreamed up—Egg Capital of the World, Dry Pea Capital of the World. Sometimes they will leave for duty in the armed services or for college, but will return like a homing pigeon to the green grass of home.

Because they have such a strong tie to one spot, these individuals have very strong egos. They may be just li'l ole country lawyers or small-town belles but they possess a strong attitude that knows how to deal with city slickers or other outsiders. Their personal outlook on life is complete and rounded; they know their world and they know their roots.

Women with this type of Life Line love local traditions and being close to Mom and all those people they grew up with. They take very personally the little things in their community and know the social barriers and pecking order. Men with this line share this interest in local history and also have a deep pride in local character.

Don't ask these individuals to move. They will not. They want to remain in the motherland. If they do move, they will get homesick, pine for hours on the phone to old friends, and use every holiday as an excuse to return to the promised land. They will never miss a class reunion.

These people are actually very supportive partners and with the right Heart Line can be very active individuals, as long as they feel secure on home soil. As a result, however, they can break out in supporter rash—a mental affliction one gets from supporting other people's dreams more ardently than one's own.

THE OUT-REACHING LINE OF LIFE: THE BOLD SEEKER

The out-reaching Line of Life (figure 32) marks a protean individual, a person who leaves home, explores all possibilities, and changes as experiences season him, yet maintains a sense of continuity. These individuals are achievers who will follow through on their ambition. Indeed, these individuals constantly look to the horizon as if gold is to be found there. But even though they may leave their hometown or neighborhood, you can't take their old environment out of them. They keep in contact with old buddies and will go home to reunions when they can.

Often a travel fork at the end of this line signals an itchy foot. Travel will be the prime way of learning. These individuals believe in the song of the open road and the Eurail pass, that to see is to believe, and that life experienced is life understood.

These are highly upwardly mobile people who have the energy and enthusiasm to go far. They are good companions and willing partners. However, a caution should be noted if this line is "chased" by several influence or interference lines from the Mount of Venus (lines which radiate out and almost cross the Line of Life, but don't because the line wings out widely). This often signals an individual who is consciously or unconsciously trying to run away from a personal or family problem.

The formula to remember is that the wider the Life Line goes into the Plain of Mars, the more the person gets into the thick of the struggles of life and the greater the chances are for travel or changes in residence.

THE NEPTUNE LINE OF LIFE: JOURNEYER

This line seems to "journey" across the palm, beginning on the Mount of Mars positive and go across the hand to the Mount of Neptune (figure 33). This is a line of the person who travels greatly in his life. These individuals may move great distances and end up living in a place very, very far from where they were born. "Born in New York, moved to L.A." is a common theme, but it is equally true of "born in Detroit, moved to Dallas." A high percentage of these individuals will spend at least some time abroad, as Neptune likes to travel over water.

The reasons these individuals travel vary from those who travel for fun and excitement to those who are moving to seek a better life, to get away from an oppressive system. This pattern can at times be seen in the hands of immigrants (certainly not all, for some are Bold Seekers) and refugees.

Usually these individuals have a very visionary or mystical approach to life. Not that they're not practical; they are—for they can be shopkeepers, tradesmen, profes-

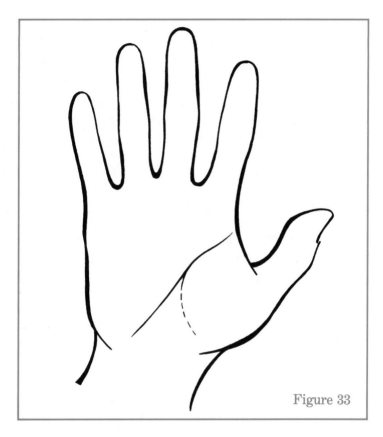

Figure 33

sional people. But they also have the vision to move and implement change. They know what they want and have the courage to seek a richer opportunity for themselves, even at the sake of great physical and emotional dislocation.

Getting involved with this person means getting involved with this vision. It will mean either periods of separation while the journeyer is traveling, or great travel for the both of you. If you embrace this lifestyle, this might be a good type for you.

The key to being a partner to this type of person is your attitude toward adventure. You have to be open to risking and seeking. This is a great type to have for a partner if you are open to the spirited call of life's possibilities.

THE OUTWARD SHIFT: THE SOCIAL HOP-UP

When the Line of Life breaks and starts out farther in the Plain of Mars (figure 34), it indicates that the individual will achieve a sudden change of life—a change that will widen the opportunities available to him for advancement and offer him a higher notch on the social ladder. Consider this the mark of the yuppie, the boy who gets a break, starts his own business and hits it big, marries the boss's daughter, buys low, and sells high. Or it could be the woman who marries "up," landing that professional man and moving into a new social set; or the woman who works hard, gets into law school, passes the bar, and leaps into a whole world outside of shopping and what to fix for dinner.

There can be more than one break in the line. I have seen as many as five, and three is not uncommon. Each break indicates another shift in lifestyle. Here is one instance in which palmistry's accuracy scores in the eightieth to ninetieth percentile;

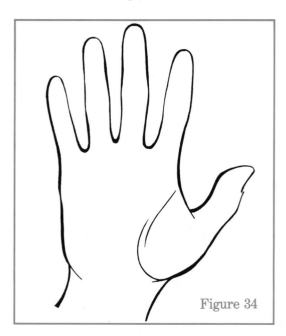

Figure 34

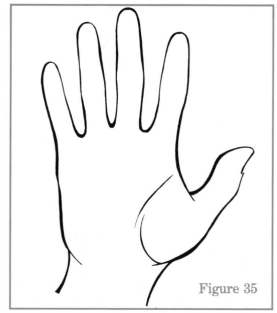

Figure 35

for it has been my experience that this configuration is very accurate in predicting that an individual will experience large shifts in his or her life.

Relating to these individuals means being able to hopscotch with them. Sadly, often it is one wife who puts the individual through law school, and another—after the first has been discarded—who quarterbacks the battles that help him become a partner in his firm. Conversely, a woman with a broken line often starts as just a sweet girl taking some night classes, when her job takes off and the old hubby who works at the mill just isn't enough anymore.

This is not to say that this scenario happens every time with this pattern, however. Individuals with this pattern can start a business and see it take off, go from three to sixty employees, make money, and move into a ritzy neighborhood, all at breathtaking speed. But such individuals must almost always deal with stress.

Friendships can be difficult with these people. Old and new friends may not mix and it may take time to sort out the different friendships. Material evaluations such as "what can you do for me?" are the issue here. Some old friends will just get lost in the shuffle of changing social strata.

Traditionally, these people are "winners" whose energy is always strong and vital. However, they often look at relationships as a complex system of meeting and knowing other winners, so they may be somewhat political in obtaining and keeping a mate.

Being in a relationship with this type is therefore like being a stock on the stock market. If your market value is high, you are praised, but lose your market value and you lose the relationship. Of course, not all "broken lines" are fickle; there are loyal types in this group, diamonds in the coal bin. Still, this type has the greatest difficulty in long-term relationships, especially if partners don't like change.

THE INWARD SHIFT: RETREAT TO A QUIETER LIFE

When the Line of Life breaks and resumes closer in on the Mount of Venus (figure 35), it indicates a change to a quieter way of life. Displaying the polarity opposite to that of the outward shift, here are the people who move from the city to the country, seeking life at a more humane pace.

This shift can also indicate a type of fast-lane burnout. In extreme cases health problems may be a factor and an individual may be forced to slow down. It may also indicate a change of job *without* a change of location. For instance, an executive may start teaching college, or a big lawyer may step into a less stressful type of law practice.

When this shift occurs at the end of the Line of Life, it indicates that retirement will be reclusive, perhaps with a move to secluded residence or different climate.

Those with the inward shift in their Line of Life usually experience and acknowledge the growing significance of sincerity and groundedness. They spurn the fast lane and go back to basics. Usually, you won't be hit with any surprises with this man or woman down the road—no restless hidden motives. He or she will often hint at feelings that reveal this longing for the quieter life much earlier than the actual shift takes place.

As to how this type will fare in relationships, the question of lifestyle preference of the partner is important. If you are someone who must have bright lights and big-city activity, then this probably isn't the guy or gal for you. However, if you share values of home and security and peace of mind, those inward breaks of the Line of Life are a good sign of compatibility.

THE MIND-OVER-MATTER LINE OF LIFE: THE SELF-MADE PERSON

This is a complex configuration. The Line of Life breaks, but begins again at the Line of Head (figure 36). Often people with this marking think they have a short Life Line because the line appears to stop. Sometimes an amateur or doom-and-gloom palmist will terrorize the person, foretelling a short life. In fact, the opposite is true. These individuals have willpower and the ability to use it to mold their lives to fit a higher form. The key to the person with this line is his or her tremendous power of the mind and will to change the position and flow of the life-force. These individuals work hard, set their goals, and achieve them. They burn the midnight oil, walk the extra mile, and crack the whip! These traits are all wonderful, except for one complication. They cannot see why everyone else can't be like them; after all, everyone has a mind and everyone can make decisions.

In romance, this attitude can prove problematic, for this type will go on the diet and lose weight and expect you to do so too. Whatever their effort, they will expect you to match it. With these sticklers, the old axiom applies: birds of a feather should flock together; you should understand and empathize with this mentality or be sure you have a strong psyche. If you are a housewife or a househusband, these willpower types will expect you to work hard at the household chores, to account for your time. They work hard and so should you.

The weak of heart need not apply. Ambition is the rule, and like those with the outward-shifting line, these folks are politically upwardly bound. They will move long distances to seek opportunities, and do what they must to get ahead. They will use their discipline to get what they want, leaving little to chance.

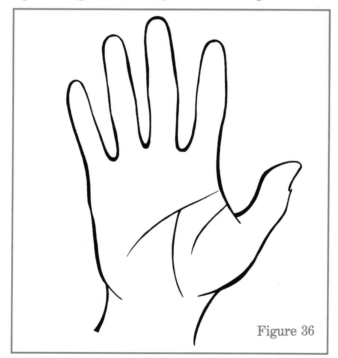

Figure 36

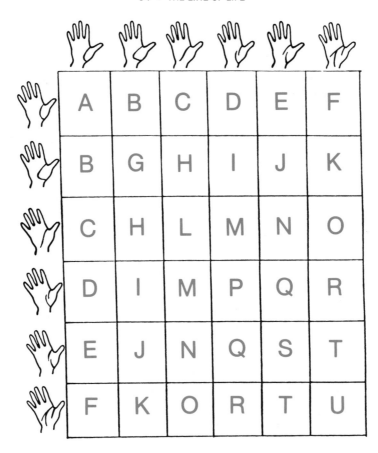

Figure 37

How do these different patterns mix when they meet on the palms of life? The Compatibility Grid (figure 37) will give you some clues. First look up your Life Line on the vertical column. Look up the other Life Line on the horizontal row. The letter where these two connect tells you where to look in the compatibility profiles that follow. These profiles grade the comparisons in terms of 100 percent. The percentage for this and the subsequent comparisons to follow should be saved for the final compatibility quotient in the "Handicapping the Relationship" chapter at the end of Part One.

LIFE LINE COMPATIBILITY PROFILES
Two Close Lines of Life: Double Home Sweet Home

Combo A

Well, at least from a geographical point of view, here are two homebodies. As the saying goes, "snug as a bug in a rug and ready to make some rug rats"—these two Lines of Life are very compatible and will have a long relationship, providing not too many other factors enter into the picture. An eye can wander in a small-town setting as well as in a big one. Still, these two individuals share a commitment to roots and the region where they were raised. One hopes that they haven't met at a college and now to return to their respective hometowns, as that could lead to complications. If one of these homebodies has to move, for business or other reasons, the success of the move will depend on how well they can stand the homesickness, or how often they can make trips back to the homestead.

♥ COMPATIBILITY: 85%

The Close and the Out-Reaching Lines of Life:
Home Sweet Home Meets the Rolling Stone

Combo B

Not impossible but challenging, this combination is very workable if the home lover stays in one place and the out-reaching one can still travel or shuffle about. The airline pilot and the stationary spouse, the sea captain and the wife at the home port—these types of combinations work best for this pairing.

Moves will be difficult, so the close individual should be prepared to be a martyr to the career of the spouse. There is a lack of political aggressiveness on the part of the close partner that will have to be compensated for by the out-reaching partner. Close one will not like going to political company parties or having loud company guests come and smoke up the happy home with cigar smoke. And he can spot "phony" personalities a mile away. He makes the home a real place of solitude and a place of family intimacy, not a company showcase. This family and home ideal must be cherished by the out-reaching partner, who ultimately must respect this virtue if the pairing is to work.

♥ COMPATIBILITY: 60%

The Close and Neptune Lines of Life: Home Sweet Home Meets the Journeyer

Combo C

This one is difficult, as the two couldn't be more different. The close one will get ulcers just keeping up with his partner. I am reminded of an immigrant couple I once read about; she had the close line and was always wanting to go back to the homeland, while he had the Neptune line and was always singing the praises of their new home. Because she was from the old country, she wasn't about to divorce him, but she made her feelings known. In this day and age such self-sacrifice is becoming less popular. Modern men have to deal with modern women, and vice versa. Most people just don't have the willingness to put up with the differences of temperament represented by the energy of these two life patterns.

There is another example of this combination seen in the saga of Odysseus, the ultimate journeyer, and his wife Penelope, the keeper of the hearth. In this situation, the close individual was able to stay loyal while the Neptune person was out fighting, conquering, and adventuring. Under the exact same set of circumstances, another mythical woman, Clytemnestra, took a lover while her husband Agamemnon was out doing battle, and ultimately killed Agamemnon upon his return from the Trojan war. Penelope, on the other hand, waited patiently for Odysseus. If you have a Penelope, congratulations; otherwise, look out!

♥ COMPATIBILITY: 45%

The Close and Outward-Shifting Lines of Life:
Home Sweet Home Meets the Climber

Combo D

Where does the climbing lead? If the ladder to success points to the top of the hometown woodpile, this is a bonfire! The close partner can handle smalltown potluck politics. But if it means they gotta move, he feels pained. Tension will develop in that the close one deplores kissing up the social ladder or big city phonies who have no sincerity or heart.

Out-Shift will want a spouse who will make small talk with the clients and fast new friends at the country club. His close partner will find this very hard.

The political tension is the greatest here because Out-Shift has a broken line; therefore, he has a willingness to break away completely from the past. Out-Shift couldn't care less about those idiots from his old high school; at his old haunts his puberty ritual was muttering a prayer to get out and find a bigger scene.

Close will not like this moving and climbing and will carp and complain, running up big phone bills at home and maybe even a big divorce settlement.

♥ COMPATIBILITY: 50%

The Close and Inward-Shifting Lines of Life:
Home Sweet Home Meets a Homeward-Bound R.V.

Combo E

A close partner's dream come true is an Inward Shift. The idea of getting close to one's roots and back to basics is very important to Inward Shift. This is a great joy to his close partner, who can be a real help, giving the support and love needed to make the transition to a slower lifestyle.

I have seen more than one couple move to L.A. with eyes full of fortune and then go back to their hometown with a new sense of its value. L.A. ate them alive, chewed them up with the soft L.A. hustle and the countless hassles that one has to put up with to make it in the Big Orange. The same is true for New York or any big city. It does not offer a life for all.

These lines represent the pattern of the return, the withdrawal from the heat of it all to the tranquility of a slower pace.

♥ COMPATIBILITY: 75%

The Close and Mind-Over-Matter Lines of Life: Home Sweet Home Meets Willpower Deluxe

Combo F

Here are problems. Not only does Close lack the cold discipline of Mind Over Matter, but also the willingness of his partner to move or change anything in life. Moving is one potential problem, but even if they stay in the same neighborhood and Mind Over Matter does all of the bashing on the home turf, Close will become embroiled in a constant hassle of struggling with Mind's know-it-all attitude and pushiness.

Should the mind-over-matter partner be a woman, then the close one will often rise to the top almost despite himself, because with that kind of firepower backing you up, you can take on the entire block.

On the whole, given the general timidity of the close partner and the aggressive, outward-seeking instincts of the mind-over-matter partner, this is a hard relationship combination to handicap for success, unless other factors of Head and Heart are extremely positive. If the Mind Over Matter is the "head" breadwinner and the close is the "home person," the partnership has its best chance of succeeding.

♥ COMPATIBILITY: 45%

Out-Reaching and Out-Reaching Lines of Life:
Rolling Stone Meets Rolling Stone

Combo G

All things considered, this is a good combination. Both have the same life energy and there aren't a lot of problems here. These two can move around together, climb the social ladder, and perform the full life boogie. They are a fun couple.

This couple has the energy to get a lot done; they can bring change to the neighborhood and leave a path of admiring friends applauding in their wake, as they move on to another town, cause, or project.

This isn't to say that the two can't have problems; obviously they can, but the problem doesn't exist in the essential energy of the life pattern. The Heart and Head Lines, the nature of the lines, and the intersections of challenging lines must be considered to see any problems. Differences in taste, intellect, or expression of passion must be examined.

Still, this is a fun pairing—the energy is positive and there is continuity and destiny. When they click, look out—there's a fast train coming.

♥ COMPATIBILITY: 85%

The Out-Reaching and Neptune Lines of Life:
The Rolling Stone Meets the Journeyer

Combo H

These two are very similar. The difference is that Neptune will be willing to take a larger gamble, a bigger move. Dynamic and outgoing, the Journeyer is a cross-culturally aware person who knows the different value systems of the many people he meets.

It is when the Journeyer becomes a nomad that there might be difficulty with the out-reaching line. The willingness to change cultures, to pull up roots and go, is a big decision. The out-reaching partner may balk at this big jump, depending on his or her current needs to move on. It will be a question of timing as to whether the impetus to move stirs within both.

Nevertheless, big jumps are ultimately fine for the out-reaching one. They like the world circuit, the larger pathway. Therefore, there is more to keep these two partners together than pull them apart.

♥ COMPATIBILITY: 80%

The Out-Reaching and Outward-Shifting Lines of Life: The Rolling Stone Meets the Climber

Combo I

The key issue to look for here is the willingness of the out-reaching one to change social status. Outward Shift is by nature or by design a climber, being the first in the family who goes to Harvard, gets a real job, opens his own business, runs for office, or joins a country club.

Out-Reaching's ideas of adventure don't always take this mentality into consideration. For them, moving to another country doesn't require a class range, and traveling doesn't always bring sophistication.

The energy of these life patterns is very similar, except that Out-Reaching has continuity; he likes his roots and isn't trying to get away from them as much as he is just following the flow of his personal energy.

In a phrase, the difference between these two Lines of Life is social consciousness; and they will have to find a meeting of the minds to deal with the past, rather than just dumping it. To have a successful relationship, Out-Shift must be willing to compromise and offer continuity to his partner, so that the social leap isn't quite so great. His out-reaching partner then feels comfortable and can deliver all the energy and enthusiasm she has for living the high life.

♥ COMPATIBILITY: 67%

The Out-Reaching and Inward-Shifting Lines of Life: The Rolling Stone Meets the Homeward-Bound R.V.

Combo J

Opposites can attract. Usually though, the life-flow patterns of these two lines are going in different directions. The Inward-Shift partner is moving toward a calmer style, while the out-reaching one wants more action. Not a lot is happening between these two unless drastic compromises are made.

Often Inward-Shift will have to leave Out-Reaching. This is a case in which one partner goes home and the other stays in the big city. It works both ways: either the woman can't adjust and heads home, *or* she makes friends, finds a job, and stays, while hubby returns to the smaller town. Either way, they'll have big problems. A compromise can be reached in which Inward Shift goes home alone to visit, but tensions usually fray the relationship, and when the cat's away, the mouse will play.

♥   COMPATIBILITY: 40%

The Out-Reaching and Mind-Over-Matter Lines of Life: The Rolling Stone Meets Willpower Deluxe

Combo K

The potential for this combination is very high, provided that Out-Reaching is able to achieve a working relationship with Mind's great discipline. This can be a great team, with great energy levels and mind-force.

Here we have the natural talent, the go-with-the-flow guy with the strong-willed wife. Or we have the lovely natural woman of growth and direction who is popular, alert, and energetic, won over by a self-made guy who has worked on and created a new direction for himself.

These two are a one-two punch. They appeal to a wide group of people and have a nice circle of friends. The problem they may have is that Mind may be jealous. The natural flow of Out-Reaching is a real popularity-winning pattern. Mind wants to feel that he has won her by hard work and is jealous of the way she warmly responds to so many other people. Similar Lines of Heart help greatly here.

♥ COMPATIBILITY: 75%

The Neptune and Neptune Lines of Life:
The Journeyer Meets the Journeyer

Combo L

The happy wanderers. While in the Peace Corps I met a couple with this combination, a couple that had been wandering the paths of the world for years. Their life together flows in a pattern of exploration, of seeking to learn new ways, different ideas, and knowledge of foreign cultures, even if only from a lot of study. Only difference of taste or opinion can cause trouble here.

There is a restlessness to a couple like this, but it is a good match. They both possess a willingness to take big risks: to travel, to move a lot, to broaden the mind by taking to the open road. This is a life pattern out on the edge, pushing, looking. Sometimes you will see this line on the hands of members of an extensive underground movement or of other individuals who move often in foreign countries. Because of this, problems sometimes arise, as these partners may respond differently to the environments they encounter and the people they meet.

♥ COMPATIBILITY: 80%

The Neptune and Outward-Shifting Lines of Life:
The Journeyer Meets the Climber

Combo M

This combination represents a difference of style and taste. Outward-Shift is interested in changing social status, while Journeyer is exploring the world and the various talents he or she possesses. The question is, are there points on which these two life patterns can agree?

If an outward-shift woman from a small town leaves home, goes to New York, and marries a journeyer man who is in oil or international marketing, and eventually moves with him happily to his various posts, the pattern is working. But what if she doesn't like all those stinky foreign posts and longs to get back to her friends in New York? Then there are problems. What, God forbid, if he wants to stay a long time in one of those vile little foreign ports! Or emigrate there?

Journeyer can be open to a lot of things, but social snobbery is not his cup of tea. Power and life's manifestations, these are his interests. The climbing aspect and the tendency to put on airs of Outward-Shift will irritate the Journeyer. This can be negotiated, but carefully.

♥ COMPATIBILITY: 60%

The Inward-Shift and Neptune Lines of Life: The Homeward-Bound R.V. Meets the Journeyer

Combo N

This is a very improbable combination. These two energies are going in opposite directions, one back home and the other toward the greater realm of the world or at least a cultural world. These matches work only in Victorian novels where the woman is "virtuous" and stays home while Sir Neptune goes out and wins the world for colonialism. Those days are over. People who can make this work should be given a lot of credit for compromise.

♥ COMPATIBILITY: 35%

The Mind-Over-Matter and Neptune Lines of Life:
Willpower Deluxe and the Journeyer

Combo O

There is a lot working together here. Both lines have an interest in power and will, change and growth. The willingness of Neptune to explore can excite the Mind partner, who is eager to discover new realms to conquer.

The problems here are of degree. How conservative is Mind? By nature Neptune will be more outgoing, more risk-taking. If these two can work out this disparity, then their strengths complement one another. Beware, though, of power struggles that could be awesome.

♥ COMPATIBILITY: 70%

Two Outward-Shift Lines of Life:
The Climber Meets the Climber

Combo P

These individuals have a lot in common: BMWs, American Express Gold Cards, designer clothes. Their attitude is to get ahead and to leave their roots behind. They don't mind moving or changing environments, changing their dress, talk, walk, or study habits.

This common pattern does not, however, indicate that both partners will agree on the aim of their climbing, specifically the scale of their endeavors. One may want to climb from a small town to a regional center, while the other aims for a national center. The key comes down to knowing who wants to change only a little, and who wants to change a lot.

The important aspect of this energy coupling is the ability of the pair to work as a team toward a new status. They will sweat over seating arrangements at their parties, talk endlessly into the night about remarks people make, the positions people hold, moves to be made.

The problem with professionals like these is that they like to trade partners like baseball cards. Divorce lawyers get rich from these individuals' propensity to exchange partners as they move through the social strata. Still, they are interesting party animals and can be lovable at times.

♥　COMPATIBILITY: 70%

The Outward-Shifting and Inward-Shifting Lines of Life: The Climber Meets the Homeward-Bound R.V.

Combo Q

This combination is like a train with engines on both ends, each tugging in the opposite direction. Hollywood has depicted this union many times: it's the story about the wallflower who gets pregnant by the most likely to succeed high school boy. They go to the city so he can get into business and next thing you know she can't cut it, but he sure can—and does—with the boss's wife!

Or there's the one about the smart poor girl marrying the wimp who is leaving town to go to college. He comes back to run the hardware store, but she stays at his college enjoying the high-life hobnobbing with the dean's son—in more ways than one.

The interests are different here. There are many variations of this pattern. Remember that one man's city can be his woman's hick town. Lee Iacocca could save Chrysler but he couldn't get his second wife to leave New York and live in Detroit. The lesson is that the outward-shift partner must learn to take the value of place seriously, as seriously as he does money or any other value.

♥　COMPATIBILITY: 40%

The Outward-Shifting and Mind-Over-Matter Lines of Life:
The Climber Meets Willpower Deluxe

Combo R

Here is a nice match, as Mind's ambition can fuel Outward-Shift to push even harder in response. Outward-Shift will appreciate Mind's control in tight spots and determination to make things happen. These two form a very comfortable life-flow pattern together, as each has the drive to greatly change his or her personality to meet a new situation.

Any problems in this combination will likely come from Mind's determination to be in control so much of the time. Comparing these two is like comparing two great athletes—the workout specialist (Mind) who has built himself up and the natural (Outward-Shift) whose finesse and ability to win at the sport are inborn. If Mind's headstrong ego doesn't get on Outward-Shift's nerves, this is a powerhouse union.

♥ COMPATIBILITY: 75%

Two Inward-Shifting Lines of Life:
Homeward-Bound R.V. Meets Homeward-Bound R.V.

Combo S

The life-flow here is in the same direction and the sentiments are similar, but is the timing right? Do both partners get their homing instinct at the same time?

This homing instinct is not a trait of small-town dwellers alone; it might be displayed just as prominently by a Chicago couple who want to get out of the city once and for all. One reason for this flight might be to save the kids from the horrors of city life. Whatever the trigger for the homing instinct, it should happen mutually at the same time for both Inward-Shift partners. When it doesn't, problems can occur. However, because the sensibilities are so alike, she may be able to understand his need to get out of the rat race long before the need becomes strong for herself. These two are generous emotionally to one another in these situations and will most often prevail through changes.

♥ COMPATIBILITY: 80%

The Inward-Shifting and Mind-Over-Matter Lines of Life:
Homeward-Bound R.V. Meets Willpower Deluxe

Combo T

These life-flows don't have to be as opposite as they may appear. Seeking a simpler life might be a great move for Mind if he agrees on the goal. The difficulty is keeping Mind on the farm once he's there. Let's give an example: farm boy in New York with inward-shifting Line of Life falls in love with Mind Over Matter, a hot New York career girl who's a little bored. She thinks it would be great to live in Minnesota, but after the first few weeks, when the real experience of the simple life sets in, she might start missing the action of the big city. Inward Shift will stay with the slower pace while Mind may or may not really take to the new simple life. This is the catch.

♥ COMPATIBILITY: 55%

Two Mind-Over-Matter Lines of Life:
Willpower Deluxe Meets Willpower Deluxe

Combo U

Power shapes the life-flow of this combination. Discipline and hard work dominate a pattern that allows these two to achieve nearly anything, providing personal competition doesn't rear its ugly head.

These two have both changed their lives by force of mind. Thus they may be too headstrong for each other, like two small-time business people trying to make a partnership and then running the business into the ground while fighting over how to manage it. If they overcome this obstacle, these two can be a real tough, upwardly motivated couple with lots of push and pull to get things done—in family, community, and career.

♥ COMPATIBILITY: 70%

4

THE LINE
of HEAD

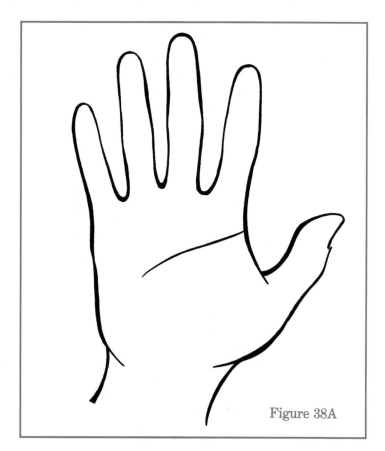

Figure 38A

The Line of Head (figure 38a) is the lightning bolt of the hand. Sometimes called the Line of Mind, it represents the electrical circuit of the central nervous system and the brain. Its dynamic position and central pathway is strategically placed midway between the Line of Life and the Line of Heart on the Plain of Mars, where the strategies for the battles of life are conceived and executed. It is the mental compass of the palm and can give significant insights into the thought processes. Considered the key to the nervous disposition, this line is like a wiring schema or a type of electrical diagram. Contrary to popular belief, the Line of Head does not indicate how smart a person is, but the way a person thinks. Some authorities assert that it can foretell physical trauma to the head, but my experience does not support this claim.

There are seven aspects you should consider when looking at the Line of Head:

1 ♥ Quality of the line
2 ♥ Small branches
3 ♥ Beginning point
4 ♥ Shape of the line
5 ♥ Length of the line
6 ♥ End of the line
7 ♥ Closeness to the Head Line

Seven is a power number. There are seven days in the week, seven seas, lucky seven at craps, seven games in the World Series, seven points of entry to the head, seven wonders of the ancient world, and so on. The preceding seven points can give you great insights into how a person thinks. Other than emotional disposition, a person's mental disposition is a most fundamental factor in how he relates to himself, the world, and his loved ones. Grasping these seven points can give you such sharp insight that you can cut through the games and discover the real core of an individual at a glance. Here is information you can really digest. With only a few experiments you will see that this line reveals amazing things to the trained eye.

QUALITY OF THE LINE

The quality of the Line of Head—its depth, and the strength of its flow—must be quickly assessed. Is it clear or is it chained or frayed, with islands, small breaks or splinters?

The deeper and clearer the line, the more dynamic the mental processes. Deep lines can hold an opinion in heavy debate. Shallow lines show a mental process that is not as strong and can be swayed by argument or by social pressure. Shallow lines are very sensitive and tuned into delicate frequencies, but do not have the power of the deeper line for cerebral combat.

Head Lines with islanding, chaining, feathering, or fraying are susceptible to nervousness and anxieties. Their flow of the energy becomes complicated and they suffer from self-doubt, introspection, brooding, and insomnia. Always look for the person with these attributes to their lines to be at least a little high-strung. This is, in part, due to twentieth-century stress, for such fraying is seldom found in the palms of individuals from primitive cultures. These individuals know nothing of paying the mortgage, a sexually aggressive boss wanting favors, bumper-to-bumper traffic, the ozone layer, nuclear waste dumps, the arms race, doctor bills, insurance costs. The difficulty of coping in modern culture manifests itself symbolically in these small imperfections of the Head Line. We see this as a static, a resistance to the pulse of the moment, often due to a heavy dose of superego and culturally supercharged expectations.

Over 50 percent of our population have Head Lines with some type of feathering or fraying. The mental tension this symbolizes can cause a stiffness or armoring in some areas of the body, and the individual who suffers from this must find a method for releasing this buildup. Possible remedies to these difficulties include self-hypnosis, meditation, yoga, and athletic exercise of all kinds, not to mention massage, stress seminars, prayer, and faith. Practice the stress reducer of your choice, but always remember to practice, practice, practice.

SMALL BRANCHES

These small lines along the Head Line, large enough to be considered spurs yet not as small as frays, should be noted. If these spurs go up toward the fingers (figure 38B), they indicate a type of optimism which relates to the finger under which the small branch occurs. For example, a spur under the ring finger indicates an optimistic attitude toward beauty or the arts, while a spur toward the little finger would signify positive communication skills. When there are two or more of these upward branches on a line, you have a real optimist on your hands (no pun intended).

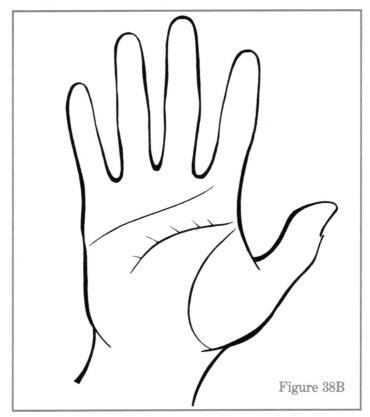

Figure 38B

When the small branches shoot toward the base of the hand (figure 39), the energy takes a dark turn, exploring what Jung calls the shadow. This individual will explore some melancholic path, explore a path not taken, or brood upon the darker questions in life. Consider the finger above which the spur occurs for a more precise meaning. If it's under Saturn, it may mean depression about the values of life, or self-judgment. If it's under Jupiter, look for doubts of ambition and leadership or career direction; this feature may also indicate a late bloomer, someone who finds his calling later in life. When you have two or more of these downward spurs, you have a very moody person, someone who will see doom and gloom coming at the first setback.

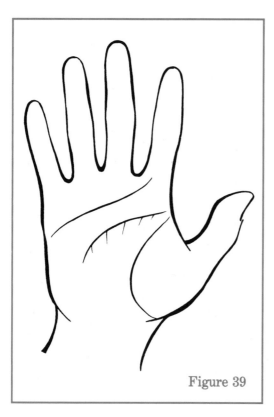

Figure 39

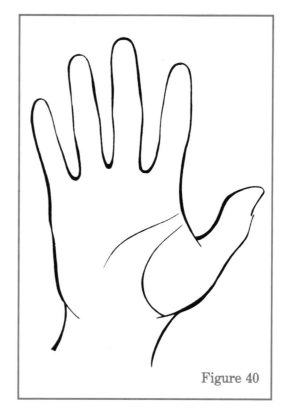

Figure 40

Some palmists say that two or more downward spurs indicate an underdog mentality, an individual who doesn't like to be the "favorite." My experience suggests that whatever else may be represented by downward spurs, mood swings will certainly accompany them.

START AT THE SOURCE

The beginning point of the Head Line is very important, so important that you must ask yourself every time you look at a hand, "Does this line touch the Line of Life near its source?" When the Head Line does not touch the Line of Life (figure 40), the person is a more independent thinker—not bound by convention and tradition, but bold, dramatic, and enthusiastic in his or her mental responses.

The wider the separation between the Line of Life and the Line of Head, the greater the independence, until a question arises as to whether this independence is actually rashness, irrational rebellion, or capriciousness.

In considering an individual for a relationship, you must know how much of a freethinker you can handle, or whether you want one at all. These "separated Head/Life Line" individuals will not be afraid to break rules, rebel against conventions, and experiment with the roles you play with each other. Sexually, this is the liberated group of individuals who express their sexual needs and often reveal prodigious appetites. Curiosity is the sexual keynote and these individuals may well point to a page in a sex manual and suggest, "Honey, let's try this one tonight—what do you think?" Or they may just spring something new on you! If you like surprises, you'll like this group!

When the Line of Head is joined with—or touches—the Line of Life (figure 41), it indicates a more traditional mental set. When the lines join for no more than a quarter to three-eighths of an inch before separating, one can expect a traditional posture and growth in the home, with a normal family life and a balance of dependence and parenting, with a growing independence. These individuals see the importance of a traditional home and traditional values, which have been good to them. They make good parents and responsible spouses.

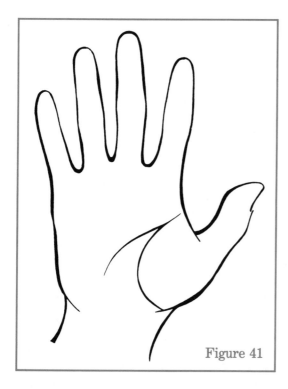

Figure 41

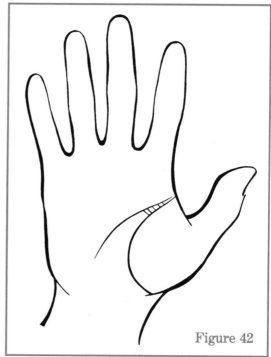

Figure 42

If there is webbing, fraying, feathering, or other breakage in the section where the two lines run together before splitting (figure 42), one can look for individuals who had trouble relating to their family, experienced sibling rivalry and growing pains, and who may be extremely sensitive about certain issues regarding their sense of self. These individuals will want to have a family in order to raise their children "differently from how I was raised." The chips on the shoulder here are manageable, though; with good love and affection a lot can be accomplished. Rubbed the wrong way, however, old wounds can open that you wish had remained closed.

When the Line of Head and Life are joined for a long time—over three-eighths of an inch (figure 43A)—you have difficulties. The family plays a very big role in this person's life, with mixed results. Sometimes these individuals are trapped by smothering parents who won't let them go. Often one finds fathers who have forced

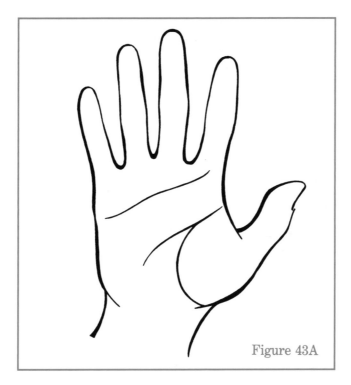

Figure 43A

their offspring into family businesses, yet won't relinquish any real power; or mothers who will decorate the newlyweds' house because she can get the stuff wholesale and knows how to decorate, while depriving the son or daughter of an opportunity to gain the experience of setting up a home. Overly dependent on the family, these individuals must be considered carefully for relationship potential. You're getting the parents as well as the individuals with this configuration, and those parents can be powerhouses with no scruples about pushing the young around—so be prepared.

Another variation on this individual is the one who, after being held back by the family for so long, explodes and becomes a rebel. Sometimes these people are bound by chores and taking care of the rest of the family; but somehow they never satisfy their parents. Their answer here is often to run away. This is especially true for those in the lower middle class whose parents saddled them with work instead of allowing them to attend college. These types are hard workers, but must be encouraged to set their sights high, especially since their parents kept them in line by putting down their ambitions.

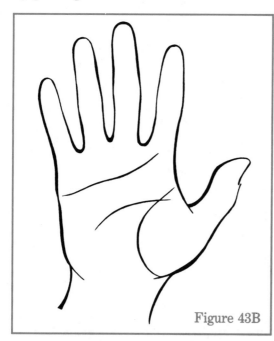

Figure 43B

Finally, let's consider the case in which the Head Line starts *inside* the Life Line on Mars Positive (figure 43B) and must cross the Life Line to get out into the Plain of Mars. This configuration often indicates that the individual must have a "showdown" with a parent or some authority figure in order to gain autonomy—to be who he or she truly wants to be. I remember one person with this mark telling me of a literal wrestling match with his father over his independence. While we don't all physically wrestle with our parents, in some way we all must come to an understanding of our adultness and separateness, our personhood, and our ability to make our own choices in the face of parental authority. There are some parents who have for years been making choices for their kids, and are loathe to stop; thus the power struggle.

Reconciliation with authority is difficult for one with this line configuration, since so much energy is spent being angry at a parent. Usually, however, a little therapy or self-examination can bring refocusing and the anger can be handled.

END GAME

The ending of the Line of Head tells a lot about the potential for perspective, or the ways of viewing a situation. A solid line ending single (figure 44A) indicates a

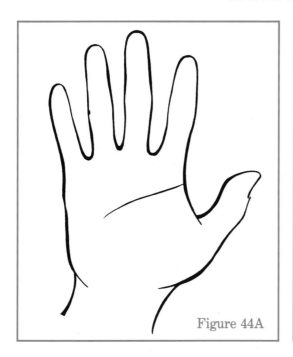

Figure 44A

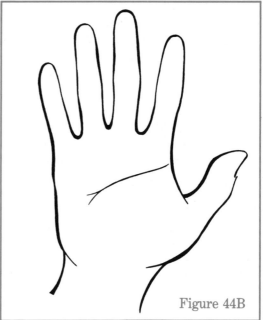

Figure 44B

one-sidedness to the individual's analytical character. This person sees things from a single point of view. When the chips are down, there is only one way to perceive the situation—his way. Those with single line endings are good at boring into a subject from their side of the fence.

Palmists tend to refer to a forked line ending (figure 44B) as a writer's fork or lawyer's fork, because writers and lawyers have to see things from two sides. Of course, one doesn't have to be a writer or a lawyer to have this fork, but the ability to see quickly two points of view is usually present. A lot of agents, stockbrokers, CPAs, and other professional types will display this mark. I enjoy people with this ending because they love to debate issues and will take any stance for argument's sake. This will disturb anyone with the single ending line who doesn't want to mess around with certain sacred cows.

A trident (figure 44C) is a very unusual three-pronged fork. People whose Line of Head ends in a trident see things differently from most other people: that is, they see both sides, plus a special dream dimension in all things. Their mental faculties are multisided. They can overestimate things enormously, yet also be the first to spot a coming trend or jump on the right idea and win the day. Their most interesting trait is apparent when they lose it all or are disappointed; at such times they are able to rejuvenate like a phoenix and rise again, or, like Venus rising on the half-shell, they are able to bathe in the sea and regain their virginity. This not uncommon but rarely noticed mark is surely one of palmistry's most interesting. Visionaries, inventors, and seers are among those you will find with this line ending.

A Line of Head split into large branches (figure 45A), indicates a person capable of swinging between two different and distinct character types. Most often one side is practical, pragmatic, and something of a pain in the neck, while the other is imaginative, dreamy, and impractical. The splits can signify a variety of things depending on the lengths of the split lines, the different areas of the palm that might be involved, and the qualities of the lines. An extra large split (figure 45B) can mean nearly two personalities!

Please do not think of this large split configuration as schizophrenic, which is a very serious psychological condition. The large split (figure 45B) referred to here simply indicates an individual with a wide polarity in his personality, whose parameters of personal conduct can vary greatly. As lovers, this type can be quite exciting, for their spectrum of experience is wide indeed. The trick is to be able to identify and work with the mood and character that is "up" and operative. If the rough-and-ready mood is up, there's no time for sweet talk—it's time for action. If the sweet one is up, the sky is the limit for romance. The problem arises when two double splits get together, because then it can be like a double date! I always counsel people with this split to get to know their sides by labeling them, like Barbara the bitch and Barby the artiste. Know by the observing ego (the awareness in you of what is happening most of the time) which personality is "up," and be aware of the energy you are manifesting; then you can handle this exciting, if difficult, personality type.

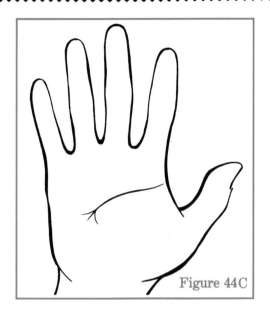

Figure 44C

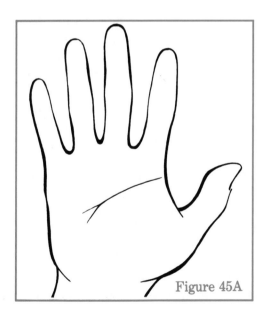

Figure 45A

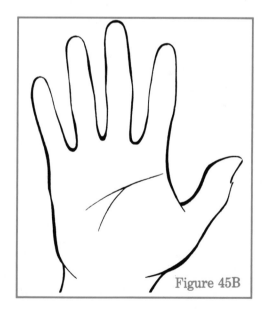

Figure 45B

MIND AND EMOTIONS

The placement of the Line of Head in relation to the Line of Heart indicates the role that emotions have in influencing the mind. If the Line of Head is pulled up close to the Line of Heart (figure 46A), the emotions can sway the mind, making thought subjective. If the Head Line seems to pull the Heart Line down from the fingers (figure 46B), then the mind controls the emotions and the individual has a lot of self-control. He can hide or guard his true feelings. A balance between mental and emotional responses is usually the best mix for a partner who can relate a full spectrum of feelings and thoughts to create a full relationship.

LENGTH AND SHAPE

Understanding the significance of the length and shape of the Line of Head is absolutely vital to reading with insight an individual's mental processes. Over the years I have developed a metaphorical technique for analyzing this line. Learn this method and you won't need to consult books or lists; you will work naturally with intrinsic building blocks, constructing your own conclusions from a growing frame of reference based on your experience. The hand will speak to you, for you know its language.

Consider that the Line of Head flows out into the Plain of Mars, which symbolizes the instinctive struggle of Life. Mars is the god of passion, aggression, and instinct. His is the energy of the warrior and the hunter who kills to feed and protect the tribe.

In romance Mars is the sexual principle, the instinctual reproductive urge, the power of the strongest males to mate—or rape—and to fight for the female they desire. Mars is the steam in the engine of love; he emerges as the protector, the provider, the reproductive urge, and pure strength. This mix contains a lot of instinct and temperament, qualities which attracted Venus to his bed. She saw in him the power of great drives, instincts, and burning physicality. Mars is hot!

The Plain of Mars represents the elemental, instinctual strengths and weaknesses of human beings as exemplified by this strong, moody god. Every society from the

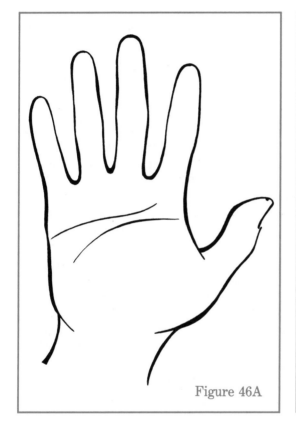

Figure 46A

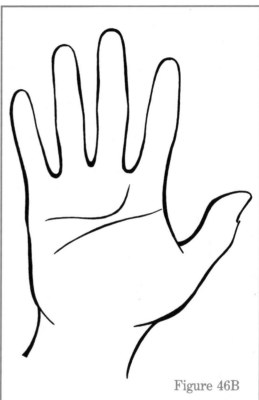

Figure 46B

most primitive to the most civilized has had to deal with the basic beast that lurks in every human. The flow of the Line of Head into this plain represents the effort of the mind to rule and control these wide-ranging instincts by the powers of reason and/or imagination. Our first rule, then, is that *the longer the Line of Head, the deeper the mind's penetration into the energies of Mars*, the more control the energies of intellect will have over those of instinct.

A *short Head Line* (figure 47A) *means that there is a high degree of impulsiveness and passion present*. The individual is more instinctive than intellectual. Do not for a minute think that this has anything to do with IQ. It has to do with the way a person uses his mind. Eggheads don't always make much money, whereas instinctive individuals often do because they don't get hung up with nit-picky things. Secondly, the person with the short Line of Head is more committed to immediate action. These individuals prefer to be doing things; they can read people, make deals, and move on. Their grasp of concepts is elemental: when they pick, they pick one or the other, and the shades of gray dissolve. Short lines work in a world of quick either/or choices. If the world is complicated, they assert, it's only because you let it be. They choose to keep it simple.

While these individuals may not be literary critics or great symphony composers, they get things done, make money, and move the economy of the planet. These people run certain trades and crafts as well as entrepreneurial positions.

Romantically, they are direct—never subtle. They know what they want and say so. "I want to talk turkey, to get the feelings out there!" If they decide to make a move, they do! They have a basic grasp on love and want some action. They can take rejection and are surprisingly successful at finding a mate.

The medium straight Line of Head (figure 47B) is a completely different type of animal. In this individual, the rational quality of the straight line is more pronounced. The line is also slightly deeper into the Plain of Mars, so the mind has more control over raw instincts. This person's logic and problem-solving abilities are strong, as is his capacity to communicate equally well with both the eggheads and the common man.

Romantically, these individuals are not as impulsive as those with a shorter straight line. They do a lot more homework before asking someone out or accepting a date. They will also plan how they meet people and usually have all their dinner reservations lined up well in advance.

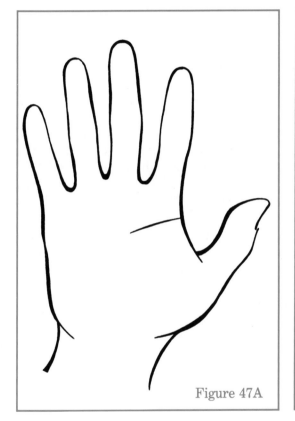

Figure 47A

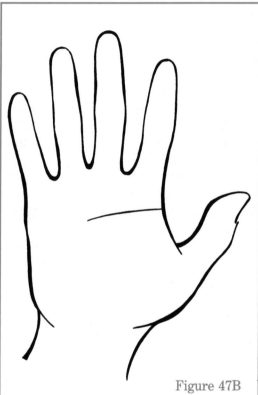

Figure 47B

All this rationalism might get boring unless you are the type of person who enjoys such predictability in your significant other. If this is true, you will be two peas in a pod.

The key is to see that *the shape of the Head Line tells you whether the mind is working with logic or imagination* to colonize and control, if you will, the vast energies vibrating on the Plain of Mars. This cerebral energy is mythologically based on the meanings of the two fingers that ride over the Head Line—Jupiter (logic) and Apollo (imagination). This can be read as a struggle of giants: *when the line is straight, logic and reason will prevail* to the extent of the line's length. In contrast, *a curved line means that the imagination is the adhesive mental energy governing the thoughts* and bringing order.

Let's consider the two extremes of the long straight line and the long curved line. The *long straight line* (figure 47C) divides the palm going from the thumb to the upper edge of the Mount of Luna. Here logic rules the hand. The intellect and will have halved the instincts, symbolized by the Plain of Mars. The credo followed here is the old Roman one: to divide and conquer the instincts. Reason will rule with an administrative will. A good memory, strong willpower, good concentration, strong logical and mental control, attention to detail, and the ability to calculate—all these subjugate the passion of Mars. Some people might call individuals with this line the cold intellectuals, the men or women of science and philosophy. They will often appear exacting and unemotional.

These long straight Line of Head types are often from another planet when it comes to love. Strength of mind struggles with the emotions, and therefore these intellectuals often have emotional weaknesses. Think of *Never on Sunday*, which is a version of *Pygmalion*, or think of countless other themes in literature in which the smart guy had to learn the lessons of feelings from a woman. This is the classic flaw of this line—more brains than heart.

Fortunately, this flaw can be corrected. These individuals, with the right heart line, are fantastic lovers. They are mentally exciting, can have charming and developed tastes in music, wine, the arts, politics. With the wrong heart line, however, they can be smart duds—you might hire them to do some research for you, but wouldn't dream of going out with them.

Sexually, these individuals are not as aggressive as those with a shorter line, but they have a real taste for experimentation and making a good time last. I remember

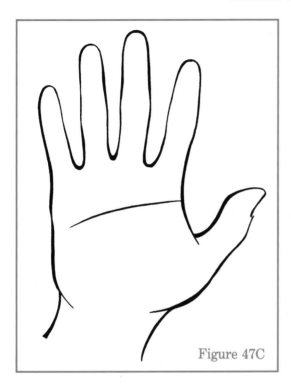

Figure 47C

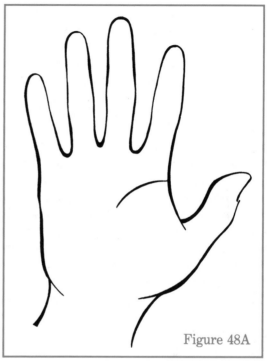

Figure 48A

telling one judge with this line that she liked costuming when going to bed. She looked at me and said, "How did you know that?"

When the Head Line curves in an arc, however, it is the imagination that rules. Reality is perceived not necessarily by what is actually and concretely there, but by what the imagination can project as potential. What is here, now, is only the beginning. When the explorers found America they saw new utopias springing up, freedoms, things which rationally hadn't existed in Europe, and they envisioned these things because they were men of imagination. Similarly, this type of person will see great possibilities in that "fixer-upper" house, the talent in the young writer, the promise of the theater project, the power of love.

The short curved Line of Head (figure 48A) signals a dynamic individual with creative instincts in the practical arena. Fifteen ways to stack the sheets, a new method to organize the warehouse, ways to make a recipe stretch to feed four more, other working shortcuts—these are just a few of the myriad ways these down-to-earth creatives can win your heart.

As lovers, these people are bold, inventive, and love to do things for you—fix your toaster or your car, sew up that loose button. Their humor is usually loud and basic. While they won't take you to highbrow spots, they do know where to have a good time. In fact, there is usually one bar or watering hole where they are well known. Income can be a problem unless they own their own business, because let's face it, they are not rocket scientists. But they *are* caring and love life. As parents, they like to be coach or campfire leader—as with anything they do, total involvement is their goal.

The medium curved Line of Head (Figure 48B) is an exciting line, for it combines the mental power of theoretical know-how with the ability for innovation within this framework. These people can be artists or inventors, men and women whose minds love to get involved with "cross-discipline studies" or comparative fields. The beauty of this line is that it can utilize the technical and logical advances of science but also creates new theoretical advances. As one UCLA professor said to me when discussing the lines, "[The comparison between the medium curved and the medium

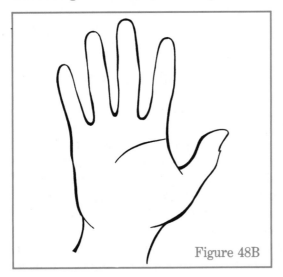

Figure 48B

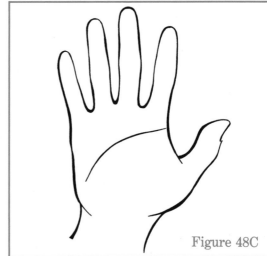

Figure 48C

straight line] is the difference between the physicist and the engineer, or the lawyer and the judge." I think an architect is a good model for understanding the powers of the curved line—creative in drawing lines, and shapes, yet knowledgeable of the laws of physics that will hold a structure up.

As lovers, these types are real pleasers. They are sensitive and know how to court and create a romantic situation. They are sensitive and innovative in bed. They can fall in love with love, however, and get bored with the day-to-day habits of "work-a-day" life. A nice nurturing Heart Line provides a goood balance.

When the Heart Line is highly romantic, there is a tendency to emotionally overcharge every situation. Small fights translate into big blemishes on the "hero" with whom they are going out. Sometimes this type is easy to win, hard to keep. Still, this line is a powerful signal—love and grand elevating passions can turn a night on the town into a journey of mystery and enchantment.

As parents, these individuals are the ones who buy the unusual educational toys, send their kids to theme camps, and actively monitor how much personal freedom is allowed at school. Often they are the ones who support their child's rights to put dirty words in the school paper or to refuse to dissect the frog. They're also likely to promote sex-education classes.

The long curved Line of Mind (figure 48C) possesses an acute visual memory. Remembering names and dates is more difficult for them than it is for the straight-lined person. The curved line remembers plots, faces, sunsets, nuances, atmosphere. This intuition is strong, as is his need to be creative and empathetic. He displays a tendency to exaggerate, and sees everything as better or worse than it actually is. He taps deeply into his imagination, which often translates into a sexual magnetism in his simplest actions. His talent brings with it a compelling need to perform in his chosen arena.

This individual can experience significant mood swings, as if the changing phases of the moon are involved (the Mount of Luna). This changing emotional pattern is like the ebb and flow of the tides (Mount of Neptune). On an up day these people can do anything, for their energy is boundless. On a down day, when the tide is out, just rustling the papers on one's desk and trying to look busy is an effort.

If you can take the emotional roller coaster ride, this type makes an awesome lover. These individuals will hitchhike across the country, just for you. They will fly to Tibet just to meet a guru. They will write you poems that are really poems.

They can make you laugh. But there *will* be times when they don't show up or cancel ("I'm sorry, I just couldn't make it") and other times when they are down and cranky. As parents they are often extreme, sending their kids to a communal school, for proper liberal training, or to that weird art school, the one where everyone has funny colored hair. For my money the ride is more than worth the price of admission, but a Coney Island rollercoaster of the mind is not for everyone.

Finally, learn to judge the amount of curved and straight qualities you see in a Line of Mind and make evaluations of your own. As I tell my students who bring hand prints to me for evaluation, "Learn to do it without me." The six types presented here are intended to open up the basic qualities of line interpretation. Some lines will run straight up for quite a ways before curving, while others curve immediately. Some lines curve and then straighten for the last third. These are all signs of exceptional combinations of creative and logical skills which must be looked at carefully and then slowly interpreted.

With the six types presented here you have the fundamentals. My own bias is that a medium length line of either straight or curved nature is the most desirable. It is dominated by the finer qualities of the mind, and yet it looks onto the Plain of Mars just beyond its reach; this mindset does not ignore instinct but is not immersed on it. The hotbed of passion that lies on the Plain of Mars appears to this individual as a place that is wild and woolly, as it were; the frontier is not totally conquered. These individuals can be highly intelligent and understand the big issues, but they can also roll up their pants and wade into the fray, following impulses and hunches, embracing the impossible or the yet unseen. Their instinctive element is active yet in control, as is their commitment to physical doing, to acting out the fantasy. It may be argued that these are the real achievers, for their mental and instinctive levels are well-mixed and operative.

Let's summarize these principles for easy recall:

1. ♥ Straight line—reason and logic
2. ♥ Curved line—imagination and creativity
3. ♥ Short line—instinct, task-orientation
4. ♥ Long line—mental control (type of control depends on shape)
5. ♥ Medium line—balance of logic, imagination, and instinct

Using these principles and remembering that the Head Line seeks to control the Plain of Mars, you will soon be ready to spot a person's mental nature long before they choose to reveal it. While performing your evaluation, remember that all seven of the significant head factors listed here can contribute greatly to your insights.

Many partners in relationships who have been with each other for years are frequently in the dark as to how the mind of the other actually works. Important issues and obstacles to happiness can be resolved with enlightenment that can come from the comparison of the Lines of Head. The following chart will enable you to compare the projected compatibility profile for different Head Lines. Look your Head line up on the left column, your partner's on the horizontal line. Then look up the combination letter in the following profiles. These are not offered as infallible conclusions, but as a way to start thinking about the mental energies represented by the Head Line and how two hands might compare. You will find exceptions to these rules, but you will find a surprising predominance of accuracies while this new way of seeing opens up to you.

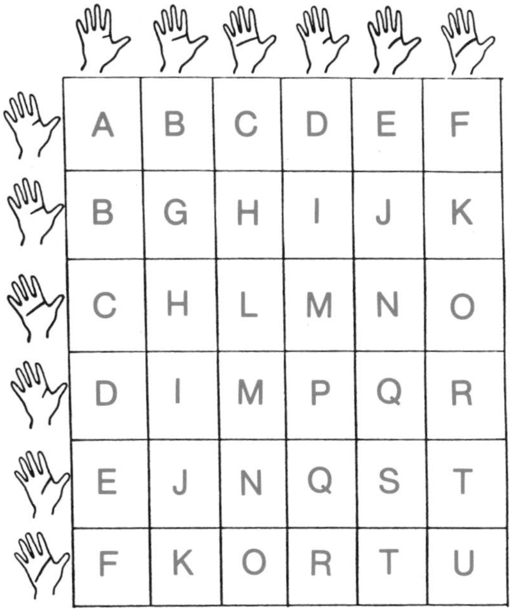

A	B	C	D	E	F
B	G	H	I	J	K
C	H	L	M	N	O
D	I	M	P	Q	R
E	J	N	Q	S	T
F	K	O	R	T	U

Figure 49

HEAD-LINE COMPATIBILITY PROFILES
Two Short Straight Head Lines:
The Expeditor and the Expeditor

Combo A

Here are two pragmatists who prefer doing something to sitting about debating issues that cannot be solved. Instinctive, energetic, and materialistic, these two can get things done. They could have good, practical business sense and above-average skills in negotiating price and terms. They should see eye to eye on tactics and methods.

♥   COMPATIBILITY: 85%

Short Straight and Medium Straight:
The Expeditor and the Technical Advisor

Combo B

Here are two similar individuals, different only in the amount of intellectualism they prefer in their materialistic perspectives. Difficulties can arise if Medium Straight decides that the energy and boldness of Short Straight is not energetic, but instead aggressive and crass. A caste or class struggle can often occur with Medium Straight playing the snob. Should this not occur, Medium Line can function as the handler of the blueprints with Short Line as the enforcer, the individual who will do extra work in the trenches to get something done. The doer is fueled by the theorist.

♥   COMPATIBILITY: 70%

Short Straight and Long Straight: The Expeditor and the Think Tank

Combo C

While both of these lines indicate a realistic and grounded nature, the voltage and breadth of vision of Long Straight will overpower Short Straight—unless Long is heavily islanded or frayed, in which case Short will help to calm Long. Short Straight is the contractor who meets Long Straight—the architect, design engineer, judge, or hot businessman. Long has to sacrifice too much finesse to the instinctive ways of Short. Barring a lot of compromises, the Long Straight Line would prefer to be less instinctive, more coolly rational.

♥ COMPATIBILITY: 35%

Short Straight and Short Curved: The Expeditor and the Problem Solver

Combo D

If these two can get the division of mental labor figured out, theirs can be a good match. The short straight line is the pragmatic problem-solver, while the short curved line is the creative one who can invent new things to do. Similarly, Short Straight is often repetitive in activities, so Short Curved can provide variety. A type of competitiveness can develop in this pattern that causes some friction, but the key to their working together is the vast instinctive energy both enjoy.

♥ COMPATIBILITY: 75%

Short Straight and Medium Curved:
The Expeditor Meets the Creative Consultant

Combo E

The pragmatist joins with the idea person, or the contractor meets the interior decorator. There have to be quite a few indications of compatibility on the hand for this one to work well. Medium Curved is interested in beauty, Short Straight in cost. One partner is interested in style, the other function. Should Short Straight have a dominant Finger of Apollo, his hard realism—or even crudeness—would likely be more palatable to Medium Curved. Generally these two individuals find it difficult to find a really reliable common ground. Short Straight considers Medium Curved an airhead, while Medium Curved considers Short Straight an unstyled bore.

♥ COMPATIBILITY: 40%

Short Straight and Long Curved: The Expeditor and the Visionary

Combo F

These two are from different planets. Sometimes interplanetary visitors like each other, but most of the time there is misunderstanding, because they breathe different gases and eat different foods. Their aesthetic sensibilities are totally different, and the aggressive instincts of Short Straight will be snubbed by Long Curved. In return, Short Straight will mock and laugh at the "artistic pretensions" of Long Curved. These two could never attend a gallery opening together without fighting over what is art: Short Straight likes art that looks like something—that is representational, while Curved understands impressionism and modern art, forms that Short insists a child could duplicate. A blind date between these two is a surefire disaster unless both parties are feeling very tolerant. And after the first night, it's all downhill!

♥ COMPATIBILITY: 30%

Two Medium Straight Lines:
The Technical Advisor Meets the Technical Advisor

Combo G

These two managers meet and fall in love based on each other's budget reports and goal projections. They love routine and can be active, but are more consistently thinkers and planners. Apt to delay reward for hard work, they can think alike, be realistic, and endure repetition. Later, however, things can become too routine and the seven-year itch can cause real problems. Until that day does or doesn't occur, these two are excellent together.

♥   COMPATIBILITY: 85%

Medium Straight and Long Straight:
The Technical Advisor Meets the Think Tank

Combo H

The five-year planner and ten-year planner meet, and like each other's style. If they have what seems to be other complementary aspects, they can work out a very strong partnership. But the problem remains that the Long Straight will consider himself the more refined thinker, the more serious planner. If Medium can accept the fact that Long is usually better at planning and better at dealing with people, these two can get along very well. However, the ego and self-righteousness of Long may get boring to Medium, who is more of an instinctive and humble person. This glitch could eventually cause bad feelings.

♥   COMPATIBILITY: 70%

Medium Straight and Short Curved:
The Problem Solver Meets the Technical Consultant

Combo I

This can work because Medium Straight finds both the life of the party and a willing supporter in Short Curved. The problem is that Curved may perceive Straight as a bit of a stuffed shirt. Still, these two are salt and pepper, energy and creativity paired with good judgment. Fighting is difficult, as Medium Straight fights with coolness and distance, while Short Curved fights with instinctive and emotional confrontations. Ultimately, this combination can work because the individuals complement each other without a lot of competition.

♥ COMPATIBILITY: 70%

Medium Straight and Medium Curved:
The Technical Adviser Meets the Creative Consultant

Combo J

This is a nice combo because the division of work is so clearly defined. Differing attitudes toward spontaneity, however, can cause strife. Medium Curved may just want to throw up her hands and take a weekend in the country, and if fuddy-duddy Medium Straight can go along with this, they are a fine match. The brains are matched, but the aptitudes are different. When detail and vision can work together, this is a golden union. If not, Curved will leave for more excitement.

♥ COMPATIBILITY: 70%

Medium Straight and Long Curved: The Technical Adviser Meets the Visionary

Combo K

If these two can agree on their distinct roles, they can accomplish more than any other combination. Straight supplies the grounding for the imaginative flights of passion that the visionary must have to express his inner soul. This is the designer and the marketing force, the inventor and the patent attorney, the egghead politician with the cunning wife. Should they not hit a deal, however, Curved Line will leave in a huff.

♥ COMPATIBILITY: 65%

Two Long Straight Lines: The Think Tank Meets the Think Tank

Combo L

The cool towers of intellect meet. These two are deep thinkers and cagey customers; when they mix the brew is exciting. They have a fantastic grasp on their reality and their situation together. Both can learn skills quickly and are great partners in a working situation. Even the slightest curve to either of these lines indicates that this is a great combination. Individuals with two *very* straight long lines may adhere so much to routine that they may be a boring couple, but this is not likely. These lines usually live life with high standards and are seen at a good many big company parties thrown for top personnel.

♥ COMPATIBILITY: 85%

Long Straight and Short Curved:
The Think Tank Meets the Problem Solver

Combo M

I doubt that these two can really get along unless Short Curved is selling a new product to Long Straight in a business transaction. The differences of thought processes are too great: while Long Straight is cool, rational, calculating, and control-hungry, Short Curved is instinctive, creative, enthusiastic, and emotionally dominated. Long Straight will dismiss Short as a brash—or at least loud—intrusion, and Short will view Long as a sawdust mannequin.

♥ COMPATIBILITY: 30%

Long Straight and Medium Curved:
The Think Tank Meets the Creative Consultant

Combo N

The cold logical one meets the creative one. This is okay if the creative one can put up with the smug tolerance of Straight, who is arrogant about his logical thought processes. Often Curved is the creative one and Long Straight is the bigger bread-winner. If the goal is to share moments and passion, this combination is good, for it makes the Long Straight a more human person. If Medium Curved gets unhappy, he may regress and act childish, spending money on foolish things or starting sexual affairs just to show Long Straight that his passion can be powerful.

♥ COMPATIBILITY: 55%

Long Straight and Long Curved: The Think Tank Meets the Visionary

Combo O

This is a coupling of polar opposites, the rational and the imaginative, the materialist and the visionary. If they can work out a divison of labor, Long Curved will have found an ideal partner who can ground and direct the energies that whirl within. In a way, though, Long Straight will appreciate Curved more, for Curved adds variety to his life. Curved may resent the ego and rationalism of Straight and want to rebel; still, this one can work wonders when it works.

♥ COMPATIBILITY: 70%

Two Short Curved Lines: The Problem Solver Meets the Problem Solver

Combo P

These two can match each other well. They are impulsive, instinctive, energetic, and creative—all with a practical eye. Any problems between these two come from a competitiveness over dominance, and therefore areas of interest must be defined. These individuals are often excellent at crafts and marketing and they may coordinate their efforts well in these areas.

♥ COMPATIBILITY: 80%

Short Curved and Medium Curved:
The Problem Solver Meets the Creative Consultant

Combo Q

These two are the same note in different octaves. They both like change, being different, and embracing new trends. One is the creative consultant, the other the creative facilitator. Differences in taste, in ideas about ways to generate change, or even in opinions about which charitable cause deserves their support may try the patience of one with the other, but these two have to look to other parts of the hand to find real problems.

♥ COMPATIBILITY: 80%

Short Curved and Long Curved: The Problem Solver Meets the Visionary

Combo R

The tinkerer meets the visionary. These two have a lot more going for them than meets the eye. In fact, Short Curved can be a great asset to Long Curved, who tends to be impractical, puts things off, and thinks too much. Short Curved will also bring action, instinct, and push to the relationship. You might consider this a meeting of the commercial artist and the abstract artist. But even though these two can be very different, they are both creative and flexible, displaying talents in different areas. The two share a love of intuition over reason.

♥ COMPATIBILITY: 65%

Two Medium Curved Lines: The Creative Consultant Meets the Creative Consultant

Combo S

The only problem here is that one of the two has to have his feet on the ground. If not, this becomes a difficult couple because they keep attempting to achieve the impossible. However, if there exists a grounded aspect (as indicated by a long Jupiter, for example, or a straight Heart Line), these couples are very dynamic, movers and shakers who get a lot done. Creative and strongly intuitive, they both have talent; they just have to keep it positively directed. Competitiveness can come into play here (who's most creative) but if these two are grounded, they fit each other nicely.

♥ COMPATIBILITY: 60%

Medium Curved and Long Curved:
The Creative Consultant and the Visionary

Combo T

This is a difficult pairing because Long Curved is so powerful and persuasive in realms toward which Medium Curved is already predisposed: spontaneity, imagination, exaggeration, ungrounded vision. These two can take off together on wild ideas and get into deep problems. If Medium Curved has a short straight Heart Line or a dominant Jupiter, then this is a better match. Short Curved may also have more realistic visions than those of Long Curved and find herself tiring of having to listen to another tale of Atlantis.

♥ COMPATIBILITY: 50%

Two Long Curved Lines: The Visionary Meets the Visionary

Combo U

These two can leave for India in a week and not come back for two years. There is a level of vision and imagination that makes these two a very interesting—if unstable—pair. As long as they keep hopping to the same mental stone in the stream of their consciousness, they can get along. However, when their imaginations don't stay in sync, problems develop. The mood swings here can be enormous, since both Long Curved lines tap deeply into the Mounts of Luna and Neptune. Things get easily distorted by both people and it can be difficult shrinking them back down to size. When this union works, it really works, but when it flops, it really flops. I suggest someone with either a straight or short Line of Head as a partner for someone with a long curved Head Line.

♥ COMPATIBILITY: 55%

5

THE LINE
of HEART

"How's my Love Life?" is a typical question palmists are asked every day. Is there a line for love on the palm? Yes. The Line of Heart is located directly under the mounts of the fingers and rules the emotional aspects of an individual's personality, governing his basic temperament as well as his romantic and sexual feelings. Gypsy palmists candidly call this the "love line" and will read it for love affairs. Some palmists claim that it also indicates important information about a person's emotional and physical health. While this may be true in some instances, it is also true that palmistry is not an exact science and no attempt to use the Heart Line to diagnose health problems will be made here. Rather, the Heart Line will be presented as a window into our passions, those feelings that psychics call the emotional body—that which fuels our chakras and auras—and shapes our interaction with others and ourselves through an energy very different from mental logic.

The key to the Heart Line is its length and shape. The longer the line, the more emotion is present. If the line is straight, this emotion is ruled by a mental factor; feelings go through a mental process. People with straight Heart Lines think before they speak, reflect before they express, and can hold back expressing feelings for the moment. They are good at what psychologists call deferred reward, which translates into seeing the profitability of a long-term investment or seeing the prize at the end of a hard task.

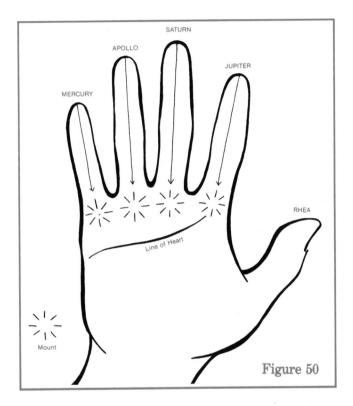

Figure 50

If the Heart Line is curved, the person is ruled by sentiment and intuition. People with these lines are "touchy-feely" and express their emotions immediately. You know where they stand because they say it, right on the spot! They find it difficult to hold back their feelings. These individuals make great motivators, for they are quite charismatic and can raise the emotional level of those around them. Tommy Lasorda of the Los Angeles Dodgers has a very curved and dynamic Heart Line and he is known for getting the most out of his team, motivating them to play to the top of their ability.

The Heart Line runs along the foothills of the mounts, the pad at the base of the fingers (figure 50). The metaphor of rain is useful to visualize how the mounts give energy (think of rain run-off) to the line. Each mount is charged with the power of the finger above it: Jupiter, ambition; Saturn, taskmaster; Apollo, aesthetics; Mercury, communication. The height of the mounts determine the "runoff" that the Heart Line will absorb. For example, if a person has a big Mount of Apollo, he will have an intense appreciation of beauty. Beauty will not be something that is merely contemplated; it will be gushed over passionately. Trips to the Metropolitan Museum will be a religious experience; sunsets will be God's evening murals.

An individual with a big Mount of Jupiter will have an ego problem, and he will be ambitious and pushy. Remember, though, that it takes a certain amount of ego to be any kind of champ. Good ball players want to be given the ball, because they are convinced they can run with it. Check out their Jupiter! Use this "Mount runoff" theory to understand the passions of the heart and you will be able to make sense out of most Heart Lines. And you won't have to memorize a long list of attributes for each mount by shape and size. It is logical to just consider each mount a little mountain ridge, contributing energies to the Heart Line according to their relative sizes and reflecting the meaning of the fingers under which the mounts lie.

If the mount is between two fingers, it combines those two energies. For example, a mount between Apollo and Mercury is a super aesthetically pleasing communicator, one who can charm as well as speak and whose perceptions about the beautiful are wonderfully articulated.

Finally a note about forks or splits at the beginning of the Line of Heart; these are rivers forking at the headwaters of the line. A fork at the beginning gives the line a stronger flow, for it draws upon different parts of the mounts, producing a blend that intensifies the basic pattern of the line. The fork usually means that there are stronger and more heartfelt qualities of loyalty, passion, or ethics present— whatever their indications of the point of origin. For example, branch going across the Mount of Jupiter would signify great pride, warmth, and enthusiasm.

In looking at the Heart Line, we'll examine six basic patterns that allow most fundamental configurations to be identified and understood. Because this line is important for evaluating the emotional quality of potential relationships, it deserves special care and attention for our purposes. This is the line that tells the most about our feelings. If you are interested in romance, this is the section to study well, for feelings and how they are both expressed and received are at the core of the Line of Heart.

THE LONG CURVED HEART LINE: THE ROMANTIC

This is the Heart Line (figure 51) of the most romantic of individuals. "Sentimental" is their middle name. The long curving line touches or almost touches (within a quarter of an inch) the base of the index finger (Jupiter). A beautiful line, it marks a person who is extremely sensitive. Such an individual has a great amount of emotional energy and wants to channel it in a romantic way. Remember that the heroic lifestyle can also be considered romantic; these individuals can often get quite carried away looking for that dream of theirs.

Often interested in music, poetry, and philosophy, these people make great companions, for they prize and romanticize friendship. They prefer happy endings at all costs, and wish they could revive some of the romantic passions and traditions

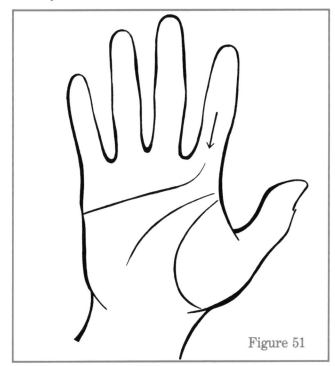

Figure 51

of the past when chivalry was still alive and "real" men and "real" woman walked the earth in the noble lifestyle portrayed in story books.

These individuals make good lovers and wonderful wives or husbands. They can idealize the role they are playing in marriage and be very supportive. One word of caution, however: if you are entering into a relationship with this type of person, recognize that his romantic ideals will often outdistance reality. His goals and dreams put his partner at a disadvantage: how can anyone live up to another's dreams? And if you should fall below his or her romantic vision, this person can be very slow to forgive. So remember, it can be lonely on a pedestal. From the very beginning, work with him on seeing you as you really are, and don't fall victim to the joy of thinking how nice it is that you have such a high, exalted position in his life. You'll only be setting yourself up for a fall. If you defuse this time bomb, you can have a great relationship with this person, as well as a wonderful time. These individuals can be true-blue, but they have to realize first that you are human, not a vision from their romantic reading or daydreams.

THE GENTLY CURVING HEART LINE: THE NURTURER

This gentle line (figure 52) terminates at least a quarter inch or more from the base of the index finger (Jupiter). This is one of the most desirable Heart Line configurations. The gentle curve indicates that the person can sense and talk about his feelings, reveal his deeper stirrings and show sensitivity to others. These people make great counselors, psychologists, teachers, managers, and nurses. They can accept people for what they are and are usually emotionally well adjusted, particularly since their emotional expectations are grounded in the realm of human possibility.

However, these individuals are sometimes criticized for not being ambitious enough. They are content, less than eager to push harder in the rat race just to keep up with the Joneses.

If they lack the killer instinct, though, they have the healing touch, a real gift. Most individuals with this type of Heart Line are good friends, honest lovers, fair parents, and sympathetic humans. Their love and support is a thing to cherish.

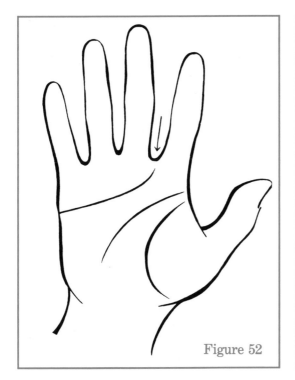

Figure 52

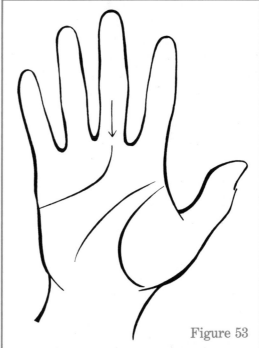

Figure 53

While they will take in stray cats, heal wounded birds, and befriend the office misfit, they can, with encouragement, also be leaders and money-makers.

THE SHARPLY CURVING HEART LINE: THE DYNAMIC

This Heart Line (figure 53) curves sharply up under the middle finger (Saturn). Look out! Here comes a hugger and a squeezer, a touchy-feely person who is very extroverted and exudes a lot of sexual energy. These people are direct. If they like you, you get hugs. If they dislike you, they'll find a way to express it.

These people are emotional powerhouses. They are spark plugs, motivators, vice presidents in charge of marketing, door openers, and self-starters. They can wear you out! They say things out loud that might make the weak heart blanch.

The energy these people have is amazing: they can make a group of people laugh, cry, or get to work on a project. They forgive easily and can overlook a lack of manners. At the same time, their tempers are awesome. Hurricanes have nothing on these emotional tornadoes. They can throw things and bowl you over!

They are also athletic, strong, physical lovers who radiate animal magnetism. Their sexual appetite is large, so make sure you are as sexually active as they are before getting locked in a bedroom with one of them.

THE SHORT STRAIGHT HEART LINE: THE PROFESSIONAL

The short, straight Line of Heart (figure 54) ending under the middle finger (Saturn) indicates a reasonable person, perhaps one who is overly so. While all straight Heart Lines are reasonable, the short straight Heart Line is the *most* rational, dominant, and self-controlled. Sometimes termed the professional Heart Line, people with this line are careful, realistic, good at planning, and emotionally disciplined.

All professional Heart Lines are good at managing people and seeing things objectively or often scientifically. But they can fall into ruts, into fixed patterns in work, play, or romance. While not the most spontaneous or open of lovers, they can be relied upon to keep a relationship going, show up when they say they will, or pull out if the emotional or monetary price becomes too dear for what they are getting.

These Heart Lines can take pressure and the heat of making big decisions. And while some people may think they are cold and unemotional, these individuals can actually be very warm after you've proved yourself to them. Straight lines tend to be testers; they want to know if you really love them or if you are just saying it.

Sexually, they are good performers, but they often like the power role in sex. They do like to keep their lovers grateful. Good providers, they are great when they are loosened up and among those they love and trust.

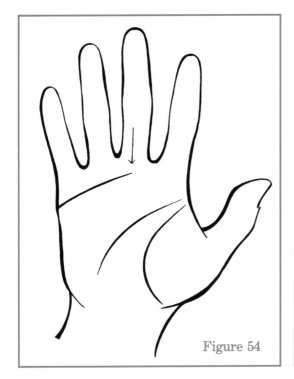

Figure 54

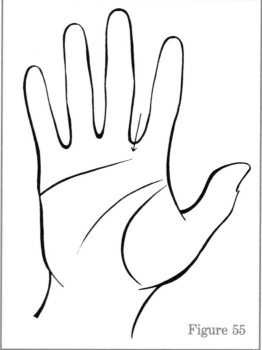

Figure 55

THE MEDIUM STRAIGHT HEART LINE: THE MANAGER

The medium straight Line of Heart (figure 55) is a pensive, emotionally stable individual with a wide variety of professional interests for which his emotional aptitude is excellent. One might call this the Yuppie Line. This person is geared toward achievement. Self-discipline is used for an end; work hard, get money, play hard, win a lover.

Good at planning, these individuals are organized. If you want a sex life in an organized pattern—Tuesday, Thursday, and Sunday afternoons, or whatever—this is the line for you.

This line is great for diplomats who must be charming and social, yet very firm and controlled in the way they interact at work or a party. They believe in goals, and ways to achieve these goals. They are the backbone of every business team.

They make wonderful parents and enjoy their parenting roles. At one time or another they'll most surely take on den mother or father chaperone responsibilities in Little League, Scouts, Blue Birds, or any other organized activities at their kids' schools. They can be pushy parents who'll drive miles to get little Sally into the right dancing class or little Johnny into an accelerated learning program at a private school. Still, honest love is here; even if it is rather structured, it is sincere and nurturing.

THE LONG STRAIGHT HEART LINE: HIGH INTENSITY

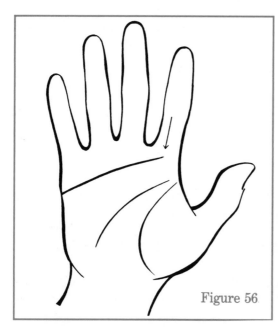

Figure 56

Be cautious when you meet someone with this long straight Heart Line (figure 56). It has so much energy and enthusiasm in it that lesser souls can be blown away in a moment. "Intense" is the catchword for this person. These folks bring a high emotional impact to anything they do.

In relationships they are very involved. They give one hundred and ten percent, so if you can't take the heat, don't go into the kitchen. They can be very possessive and any infidelity will create a huge crisis.

On the flip side, they are loyal, protective, and supportive to the point of nearly carrying the ball for you. That's why in work situations this type is often found as the right-hand to the company president —the low-profile pinch hitter who usually does most of the legwork. There can be great rewards for you with this one in support of your goals, *if* you can handle the emotional push they bring to everything.

"Smothering" is a word that can be used to describe some of their love involvements. They will want a list of what you ate for breakfast, which bus you rode to work, an outline of the people you talked to throughout your day, and a complete breakdown of your lunch hour. While this sounds like a lot, those who can deal with this person will receive love, ideas on what to accomplish at work, and staunch support in office politics.

Often this individual will have exaggerated reactions in his or her parenting role; there are tears if the Little League team loses, great joy if it wins.

Sexually, this line is great as long as the environment is safe. If you must, buy a lock for the bedroom door, for that little lock is your key to one good time. Individuals with this line can be dynamos of love as long as they feel secure.

A word of warning about the long straight Heart Line in any domestic arguments. These people can really bear down on a topic and it's best to set some simple rules for limiting arguments to a set number of hours. Otherwise you'll find that partner with this line can get as much release out of arguing as he does behind that locked bedroom door!

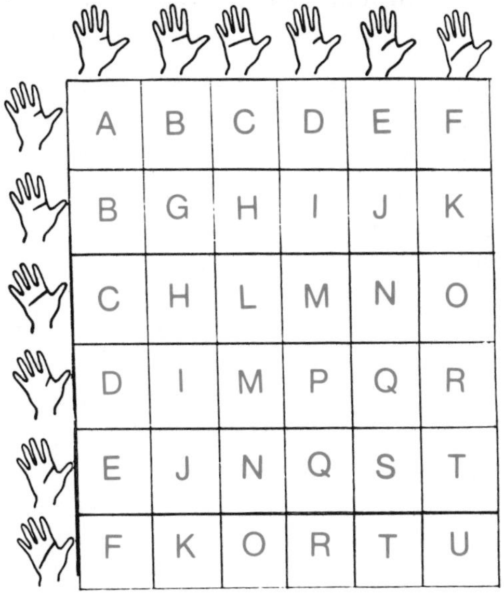

A	B	C	D	E	F
B	G	H	I	J	K
C	H	L	M	N	O
D	I	M	P	Q	R
E	J	N	Q	S	T
F	K	O	R	T	U

Figure 57

HEART-LINE COMPATIBILITIES

The following chart compares the ways that the six basic Heart Lines we have just explored will interact with each other. Look up the number one Heart Line on the left column, the other on the horizontal row. The letter they share in the grid indicates which analysis to look up in the following compatibility profiles.

Two Long Curved Lines: The Romantic and the Romantic

Combo A

Despite similarities, this is not always an easy combination. There is the possibility of great heights, great gestures, sweeping emotions, and poetic feelings. Yet there is also the chance of premature burnout and attempting the impossible. These individuals must learn to exercise some realism in their emotional gushing, or they will find themselves drained and the relationship over before they know it. We only remember Romeo and Juliet because they died young. When control is exercised and a bit of planning utilized, the natural, spontaneous, and idealistic feelings of these two lines can yield the highest form of sublime love. When a common religious feeling, meditation, or philosophical belief is shared, these lovers are bound by a higher love and greater consciousness. This grounds their nature in a rock of spirit that gives a foundation to what they see as ideal. These birds can soar over mountains, or get stuck in the tar pits. Insight into the self is the key. Know you are a romantic, revel in it, but be careful where you let your feelings soar. You can project an epic where a sonnet will do.

♥   COMPATIBILITY: 65%

The Long Curved and the Gently Curving:
The Romantic and the Nurturer

Combo B

A lively couple. The possibilities here are very good, for the nurturer is easily able to give some real support and growth potential to the emotions of the romantic. The difficulty is in getting Romantic to view Nurturer for what he is, rather than as a projection screen for a lot of wild fantasies. Also, Nurturer must be careful not to take on the parental role of raising Romantic as an emotional child by directing his or her affections and growth. Such boundaries can poison a relationship, and often when these relationships fail it is because a child/parent identification has gotten out of hand. Watch for the relationship where the couple seriously call each other "Mommy" and "Daddy" in a way that does not relate to the kids. Or watch the pet names that come into play in these relations, like "Princess." When handled properly, the energies of this combination are sensitive, sensible, and rewarding, like a plane with both wings and landing gear.

♥ COMPATIBILITY: 80%

The Long Curved and Sharply Curving: The Romantic Meets the Dynamic

Combo C

This is Zeus and Hera, the roaming eye and the romantic spouse, the locomotive and the finely built watch. The sharply curved dynamic Heart Line can be exhausting to the Romantic. Romantic is interested in ideological energy, Dynamic in raw energy. Romantic wants to "make love," Dynamic wants to just "get it on." Romantic is not well armed against this emotional bruiser. The problem is a lack of a common threshold of guilt on the part of the Dynamic, who is short on table and bed manners, but long on aggressiveness. It is the Romantic who is at risk and must really hold out on having sex until the other acknowledges something special in the relationship. Otherwise the Romantic will be just a niblet for the Dynamic in the smorgasbord of

life. When a deal can be struck between the vision of the Romantic, which enhances life, and the energy of the Dynamic, which makes that vision work, then the interaction of these two types can build a dream house instead of a one-night stand.
♥ COMPATIBILITY: 65%

The Long Curved and the Short Straight:
The Romantic and the Professional

Combo D

This is difficult pairing, for the Professional Heart Line will seem too controlling and cold to the Romantic. The attraction for Romantic is the stability of Professional, who in turn likes the spontaneous and idealistic emotions of the Romantic partner. It is when the old clock on the wall starts to tick that the difficulty begins, for each will be shocked to learn that the other is really "like this all the time." When definite roles can be seen and accepted (especially on the part of Romantic), then this relationship has a good chance to bear productive fruit. The danger, however, is that a parent/child type relationship can begin resembling that of a spirited bout in a boxing ring. Complementary use of emotional energy must be employed. Romantic's enthusiasm and optimism will help to soften the basic critical nature of Professional and Professional's wisdom can help keep Romantic from scraping his knees.
♥ COMPATIBILITY: 55%

Long Curved and Medium Straight:
The Romantic and the Manager

Combo E

This is the fruitful relationship, for the Manager understands and really appreciates the strengths and weaknesses of the Romantic. The question is, will Romantic

understand the realism of Manager? Manager wants to think ahead, as in "we can plan a romantic weekend." Romantic wants to do it now. The same will apply to spending money. But of all the straight Heart Lines, this is the one that can mix best with the Romantic, for the Manager is the most sensitive of the straight Heart Lines and the one most capable of relating to the needs of the Romantic. Hopefully, the Romantic will find in this Manager Heart Line type a friend who becomes a lover and possibly more. The fireworks in the beginning may not be spectacular, but payoffs in the long run of this relationship are likely to be worthwhile.
♥　COMPATIBILITY: 80%

Long Curved and Long Straight: The Romantic and High Intensity
Combo F

Look out: this is another version of the romantic and the skyrocket! This is the coupling of the dreamy with the raw nervous energies. The high intensity individuals can do anything; when they meet up with fanciful Romantics, get ready for a fireworks display. These two soar, they crash, they fill the sky with an incandescent glow. The key word for what is needed here is control. Romantic is a flirt, while Intense is a very possessive emotional type, so the fires of passion are already bubbling whenever these two go to any social event where the Romantic can flirt. High Intensity is no wallflower, but he is not a conversationalist who likes small talk. Meanwhile, Romantic is into a lot of posturing. Obviously, jealousy can be a problem here, and Romantic must deal with the jealousy of Intense.

Both have the energy to move mountains or change the neighborhood. When united in social or romantic action these two are unstoppable. United to get personal projects done, they are just as great. But the fact remains that the energy between them is volatile, and when they argue—wow, sell tickets for it. It definitely will go fifteen rounds and bring in huge cash receipts. When self-awareness comes to a couple of people like this—usually after a failed marriage and a couple of painful love affairs—then they are ready to channel this enormous energy reserve. Unfortunately, couples like this sometimes unite for a political or personal cause, which binds the two of them tightly, but makes it difficult for their friends and for onlookers who may be of different political persuasions. Still, when this energy is channeled in such a way that other parts of their lives are balanced, the Romantic and High Intensity are the ultimate spearheads for any good cause. The minglings of these two types is like the early jet was to aviation; once their juices are fired up it takes a special airport to land them. Both parties should proceed with caution for best results.

♥   COMPATIBILITY: 65%

Two Gently Curving Lines: The Nurturer and the Nurturer

Combo G

The helper meets the helper. This is a very good combination. Both individuals are very supportive of the other. They will help the other with tasks, projects, personal goals. Any sex problem is worked out in an environment of understanding and love. The problem is that this coupling is a little bit like Boy Scout Master Meets Girl Scout Master. This sincerity is heavy and the attention to what's good for this world is high. Not that this is bad, but it isn't the kind of tension that makes for romantic novels. It is more like Mr. and Mrs. Group Therapy shifting into their I'm-Okay-You're-Okay vocabulary. Still, with the only drawback being that too much of a good thing can boomerang, this couple is one of the finest examples of human caring and interaction. If sometimes it has the flavor of pop psychology cotton candy, remember that this particular brand of cotton candy won't rot your teeth. And never underestimate the strength this combination has to get their goals accomplished. Together they are more than the sum of their parts.

♥   COMPATIBILITY: 90%

Gently Curving and Sharply Curving: The Nurturer and the Dynamic

Combo H

The interaction here can be a lot like Schoolteacher Meets Super Salesperson. This relationship can grow with both gaining something: the teacher gains energy and the ability to open up to risk, the dynamic the need for discipline, more sympathy to others, and the need to stop and smell the roses. Sexually this can be an exhausting relationship for the nurturer—the dynamic's need to be personally and sexually active on a daily basis will need to be discussed. The body can take only so much. Still, Dynamic can learn a lot about channeling energy into activities that yield higher satisfaction—coaching kids after work, taking on PTA responsibilities, and other ways to put the energy to use aside from sex and bashing heads at work.

The nurturer benefits from extra energy received from the aura of the dynamic. Just being around Dynamic can charge you up. These two can heal each other; the support and care of Dynamic by Nurturer is great, like pulling the thorn out of the lion's paw. And the push and power of Dynamic makes Nurturer feel stronger and more willing to risk what it takes to become all that his or her potential allows. This relationship is like that of a kite (the nurturer) and the wind (the dynamic): with the right balance they can soar high. Without it, their flight plan is erratic, and they may crash. Here's to the tail of the kite!

♥ COMPATIBILITY: 80%

Gently Curving and Short Straight: The Nurturer and the Professional

Combo I

The best way to view this combination is Growth Specialist Meets Bottom Line, or Sensitive Meets the Numbers Person. The problem is that the professional Heart Line is very objective and critical, quick to evaluate people and situations, slow to express feelings, and big on evaluating data. The nurturing Heart Line sees potential everywhere and wants the whole world and everyone to just get off their asses and grow. The nurturer sees the professional as cold and materialistic, while the professional sees the nurturer as almost as mush-headed as the romantic. However, this is not to say that these two cannot find happiness together. The key is for Nurturer to see that Professional has a reason for thinking about the bottom line and that this reason must be dealt with in reality. Someone has to pay the rent. Professional must also see that the drive, ideals, and sentiments of Nurturer can affect reality. Little old rams do knock down that dam with their high hopes. When these two

Heart Lines learn how to use each other's strengths to augment their respective insights, the professional will open up and the nurturer will see the need to be more realistic. The professional can be the seeing-eye dog to the nurturer, pointing out dangerous traffic that she might not otherwise have seen. And when the professional opens up to the love of the nurturer, it is a beautiful sight to behold.

♥ COMPATIBILITY: 75%

Gently Curving and Medium Straight: The Nurturer and the Manager

Combo J

This is a good combination, for it combines the best of both straight and curved Heart Lines at a middle-of-the-road level. Neither of these two individuals is an emotional extremist; they have only slightly differing world and romantic views, are both able to see the benefit of working and negotiating with the other, and seek moderation and compromise for the sake of progress.

These people are very good at creatively structuring their relationship, planning times for closeness, and allowing room to grow. They are usually monogamous and practical and thus generate long relationships. They can take quite a bit of intensity before they get hot under the collar, so the sins of the other can be forgiven without a grudge.

The problem here is that all this wonderful planning and forgiving can go flat, and instead of a romance, the partnership becomes a series of planned events that can produce an enervating effect. They become that old couple before their years, and thus must constantly take the pulse of their relationship to make sure that they haven't planned the life right out of it. As compatible as these two are, the nurturer must be able to nurture, and if the pulse has ceased, she might just slip out of the relationship to nurture someone else.

♥ COMPATIBILITY: 80%

Gently Curving and Long Straight: The Nurturer and High Intensity

Combo K

This combination is difficult. The intense partner can be so hyper and so demanding that the nurturer may become bored with the whole thing. Nurturer needs time to be with lots of people to spread his love around. Intensity's possessive attitude and his drive to have most of that energy focused on his problems can be oppressive. Still, this couple can find happiness when the exchange of emotional strengths is seen clearly: energy for understanding, freedom for trust. High Intensity just needs to learn to back off. The challenge is for the nurturing Heart Line to teach the trust that will enable this to be possible. When this lesson is learned, this couple can have an unbeatable combination of high energy and control, which will enable the relationship to grow and the couple to share lives that are directed, confident, supportive, and fulfilling. It takes work and insight into the sensitivities of the other, but it is possible, and when achieved this couple will taste the fruits of life and love very deeply.

♥ COMPATIBILITY: 70%

Two Sharply Curving Lines: The Dynamic and the Dynamic

Combo L

This combination is a real powerhouse. The sex is great, the enthusiasm wonderful. This team of prize ponies can run with the wind, pulling the chariot of their relationship along with them. They can spearhead political causes and be the force behind charitable organizations. They are parents who experience and live through the growing years of their kids, and as a result are sometimes a little too pushy with the kids, especially regarding the things in life they feel they themselves missed out on.

Are there problems that this couple can have? Yes. Power plays. These two types of Heart Lines want power: sexual power, monetary power. They can get into real wars and with the emotional ammo they have to toss around, the fallout can be great. Fights can be physical or very loud at the least. Still, I find this combination very exciting, and rewarding, for the commitment is to action and getting something to develop from the emotional to the real. Real love shows itself in real ways. It's just that when these two locomotives collide that the impact can be awesome. These individuals need to work on negotiating techniques for their arguments and developing a greater tolerance for differences of opinion. They are used to winning debates, but who can win when debating a mirror image? When balanced, they make a great couple.

♥ COMPATIBILITY: 75%

Sharply Curving and Short Straight: The Dynamic and the Professional

Combo M

Professional can deal with Dynamic; both are powerful, but in different ways— one as a reasoner and objective person and the other as an emotionally strong and dominant person. When they pair off the results can be rewarding, for the dynamic partner is the ideal door-opener, schedule-maker, project-joiner. The professional partner then becomes the door-closer, schedule-assessor, project-evaluator. They are the one-two punch. Sexually, the professional loves the dynamic for his push and drive—he tosses you into bed. The dynamic likes the toughness and power of the professional. The difficulty is when strengths become weaknesses—when Dynamic wants more emotion out of Professional, or when there is a real difference of opinion: this is the showdown. Both are powermongers who want to win. They can lock horns and really push. The only real saving grace here is that both need to get to a solution quickly, for they want action as much as they want to be right. On the whole, given the difficulty these two types have with other Heart Line types, this combination has a lot to offer. The rewards are great, and the values are similar. As the old saying goes, "No guts, no blue chips." This couple could surely rake in the chips.

♥ COMPATIBILITY: 70%

Sharply Curving and Medium Straight: The Dynamic and the Manager

Combo N

This is a good relationship when properly balanced. The dynamic Heart Line may be a threat to the managerial, but it also may not. Dynamic's energy, drive, lusty needs, even crude behavior and wanton sexual ways could throw the more sensitive managerial line off—but only for a moment. The key aspect of the manager is that he uses and controls feelings. When Manager sees that Dynamic will respond to some types of control, a real partnership is struck, but *only* when Dynamic can also see the trade-offs that are being made.

Dynamic will always be bringing people to Manager to meet and get to know, initiating the social calendar and getting the couple out on the town. Fighting is a problem here, but less so for Dynamic, who has tons of power to unload on Manager. The manager must be able to weather these storms, for the energy of the dynamic can be awesome. Still, with this consideration out of the way, this couple can be a lot of fun. They complement each other, using and growing through their different strengths. It is when they learn through experience how to utilize these differing views and to trust the other's judgment in certain matters that this couple really starts making headway.

♥　COMPATIBILITY: 70%

Sharply Curving and Long Straight: The Dynamic and High Intensity

Combo O

This is a potentially crazy relationship. Not that it can't work, but it will be one of those couples about which you always wonder, "How in the heck did they get together and how do they stay together?" Most in this combination don't make it. Dynamic dies of a headache while Intense dies of physical fatigue. The mental/emotional energy of Intense and the physical/emotional energy of Dynamic make for a very draining situation. Sex here can either be great and plentiful or sporadic and very hot, the product of the intense partner's hang-ups. The high-intensity individual can have certain rituals about sex that limit him, but when it happens, the earth moves. The Intense is usually the loser in breakups here. It takes him longer to adjust to loss, and he's slow to heal. The dynamic must learn to think more with an Intense mate; what they have to offer is rare and potent, like a liquor that you develop a taste for. When balanced, they function as a combo, the highly tuned feeling of the intense opens the door for the emotional wallop of the dynamic. Dynamic must learn to control the wandering eye, as Intense likes monogamy and becomes jealous at the bat of an eyelash. Think of Zeus and Hera and you'll get the picture. But remember, they *were* king and queen of the hill.

♥ COMPATIBILITY: 55%

Two Short Straight Lines: The Professional and the Professional

Combo P

This couple has great chemistry. The independence and rational capabilities of the professional Heart Line combination is very interesting. It produces relationships in which there can be separate vacations, long periods apart for career or political reasons. Meanwhile, the neighbors will shake their heads and wonder if there is any blood and fire in "that couple." There is a lot of tolerance toward the other, an openness to allow each other a lot of space. Rumors of affairs and other interests may occasionally fly up, but the fact remains that here is a relationship bonded in the true grit of trust. They can weather most storms, and always return to each other; the contractual partnership aspect of their commitment remains strong in the face of all sorts of tests.

In couples like this each partner has a separate sphere of influence, his or her own world. Yet each will find in the other that solace of deepest understanding. Like eagles they mate for life, share a nest and food, but spend hours flying alone— separately hunting. The greatest risk here is a slow erosion of the tie that binds, because the possibility of power plays and personal ambitions splitting this atom does exist. Like any atom, when split, the explosion erupts with great power. Still, that same power glues these two Professionals together in relationships and courtships that last a very long time.

♥ COMPATIBILITY: 90%

Short Straight and Medium Straight: The Professional and the Manager

Combo Q

Sounds like a business school reunion, but not exactly. These two types of Heart Lines are birds of a feather, except for the lust for power that the professional can generate—an energy that the manager can see as overly manipulative and abrasive. Both Heart Line types are grounded in rational responses to emotions; both are more apt to think before speaking and share an ability to take the heat.

The sex is interesting here, for the mind stimulates the emotions in this couple. Videos, games, and gadgets can all be used in this relationship, for these partners are thinkers and will see sex as a big steak to be cooked up several ways. Also, these two can plan to have sex and wait for it, then really deliver, something which drives many of the other Heart Line types to anger. What this combination lacks in spontaneity, it makes up in reliability.

This coupling can produce a stable relationship quite easily. However, there are trials. Manager may resent the power plays of Professional. The emotions may dry up, and while the contractual aspects of the relationship continue, playing with someone on the side may become an option to either the manager or the professional. Still, the capacity to handle emotions and to make up after a fight is very strong and positive here. Commitment is taken as law and is observed carefully. The long term is always the concern, and these two can find great strength in their deepest sharing and understanding of the tie that binds.

♥   COMPATIBILITY: 75%

Short Straight and Long Straight: Professional and High Intensity

Combo R

The two polarities meet in this match and the outcome is rough on the intense partner. Here the great irresistible force meets the greater immovable object. The professional's controlled tactics with his measured, logical actions are opposite those of High Intensity, who can expand more nervous and emotional energy in one evening than Professional will in a week.

The difficulty is that the Intense partner is no rival for the Professional at infighting. The professional has the control to fight close, not press, let things drag, and allow time to take its toll. The intense mate will want to talk about something *now*, but the professional will be busy and volunteer that whatever it is can be discussed *later*. "Later" is not in High Intensity's vocabulary. She loves to drive fifty miles through a storm to talk about a problem. She will lack the patience and toughness of Professional, who can make hard decisions, unemotionally, all the while doodling calmly on a sheet of paper.

How can this combination work? It is hard, but as a coordinated team, they can make it sail. Professional should be viewed as Chief Sitting Bull and his intense mate as Chief Crazy Horse. If the intense partner can realize the strategic genius of the professional and the professional can appreciate the emotional intensity of his mate, a framework for accomplishing things can begin.

Notice how a flag (Intense) waves in the breeze (emotions); notice how the flagpole (Professional) hardly bends. In this relationship, it is the flag that tatters from wear and stress. High Intensity is therefore often the loser here.

♥ COMPATIBILITY: 40%

Two Medium Straight Lines: The Manager and the Manager

Combo S

This is comfortable, like individuals of the same astrological sign getting together. There is a feeling of inner knowledge of the other, for the other is just like you! This is the diplomatic couple; each manager likes to know the protocol set by the other manager's behavior and will react accordingly. The real problem is getting the spark of romance to start—so often these two may know each other a long time or even work side by side before going out. Reasonable emotional reponse is the byword here. Long engagements, a willingness to let feelings sink in, to be "sure," are the normal courtship modes for them. This may seem bland to others, but to this combination, this is the honey of life. They will savor gifts and quiet moments for a long time. They will not burn up in a passionate relationship; instead, they'll keep the fire glowing.

Sex is seen as an earthy and wonderful act, but it can be postponed until that work brought home is finished, or even till the weekend. Not that these individuals aren't at all passionate, but they have managerial priorities and they follow the shopping list they keep in their heart. Often a two-career family, these two managers negotiate rules with one another about their needs and how they work these things out. Sound boring? Not to them!

This couple is the pillar of the community, the foundation of reason in the neighborhood. Getting lost in the comfortable pattern of routine is a danger here, but they could live next door to you and you'd wish your relationship was as strong as theirs. In any case, this may very well be a pairing of the future. Some might argue that they are like robots, but more would agree that this is the self-actualizing couple. One thing is for sure—they know how to make the ice cream cone last a long time.

♥ COMPATIBILITY: 90%

Medium Straight and Long Straight: The Manager and High Intensity

Combo T

This combination can set up a test of wills. The nervous energy of the intense mate will test the ability of the manager to stay calm, cope, and direct the energies of this relationship. When High Intensity can trust Manager's judgment, then the bridge has been crossed and the relationship can grow. By nature the intense partner overreacts to situations, just as the Manager's reaction is to be rational and evaluate the other's behavior. The energy of the intense mate is the key to a sex life that will really excite the manager. This power of the intense partner will be the wind in the sails of this relationship, while the manager will be the rudder, keeping the craft off the shoals.

The high-intensity Heart Line can indicate possessiveness, but the manager's Heart Line usually signals discretion; thus, as a rule, this couple can work out most problems if there is that initial trust and attraction that makes the process of defining the relationship a challenge in loving rather than a limiting task.

When properly harnessed, the laws of energy and reason make for a relationship in which both participants get a lot out of the union. When arguments occur, the problem will be in getting the Intense mate to clamp down and discuss things. The other challenge lies in keeping nit-picky Manager from needling his partner, Intense. If these challenges are met, the flame of love will continue to warm the pot. When this give-and-take is mastered, there is also peace and harmony. Then look out, for this combination can go places.

♥   COMPATIBILITY: 60%

Two Long Straight Lines: High Intensity Meets High Intensity

Combo U

Strangely, this combination either explodes in courtship or goes on to bond in the most remarkable manner, producing very active and determined couples. The extreme energy that exists here makes initial contact highly flammable, like "putting out the fire with gasoline." Still, there are similar energies here and if the couple does survive the threat of early burnout or backfire, what remains is very strong and enduring. Those that survive the entry heat become very tight, an "ego de deux."

Once a commitment level is reached, the vows are those of blood. The intensity that they bring is superbonding. They spend lots of time together, don't stray much—if at all—and are both fiercely protective of their offspring.

Sex is deeply felt and often referred to as "sacred." Sex is a religious rite; cheating is unthinkable, punishable by death or lawsuits and accompanied by a passionate fight to prevent the adulterer from ever seeing the kids. This combination has the messiest of breakups.

Like those of the dynamic Line of Heart, these individuals are high-energy door-openers; as a couple they work hard for causes they *believe* in. They are not always rational about their causes, but they are always emotional. They are willing to take on City Hall together. Think of this couple as a nuclear-powered vessel that runs on an energy few others have. For this reason, they are to be respected and honored as a powerful resource, people who offer insight and care. More than any couple this pair needs to have physical disciplines: tennis, golf, running, yoga. It is the safety valve that lets off just enough steam so the engine will run and not explode.

♥   COMPATIBILITY: 70%

6

HANDICAPPING the RELATIONSHIP

Evaluating a relationship's prospects is not an easy task at best. There are romantic and emotional forces that can lead one into blind alleys. And while a relationship is not a horse race, it does involve competing human needs seeking to be met.

Conversely, we like to repeat old clichés claiming that there are no winners and losers in the game of love—for being lucky enough to play such a grand game is reward enough! Yet we also know this mentality is misleading. In the quest for love there are many pitfalls that lead to heartaches. The best advice I can give is to develop your own evaluation expertise, your way of objectively looking at how a situation or relationship will work out. Some people won't date smokers, drinkers, salesmen, defense contractors, nudists, or anyone that pushes certain negative buttons. This is the bad-habit-screening method.

The approach I am presenting here is based on comparing the qualities of the dominant hands of two individuals; a method that can be used in "handicapping" any sensitive situation. It is a numerical way of using the different tools given throughout Part One of this book. You can use it for yourself and your date, or you can evaluate prospects for your friends and their dates. Get a pencil and paper, and get ready to jot down a few numbers. Isn't a strong insight worth a few calculations?

THE METHOD

First: Add up the percentages in the comparisons between your hand and your love interest's hand given in the chapters on Hand Shape, Life Line, Head Line, and Heart Line on the sample score sheet, and determine the average for Score A. Here is an example of one pairing:

Hand Shape:	*70*
Life Line:	*60*
Head Line:	*55*
Heart Line:	*+ 70*
TOTAL:	*255*
Average:	*63 (255 divided by 4)*
SCORE A:	*63*

Second: Take your thumb and finger scores. This is a subjective number—I recommend 40 for your thumb and 40 for your fingers. Add these two together and your total is 80.

Then take your subject evaluation of your love interest's thumb and fingers and add them together. (You may wish to go back and review this method in chapter 2.) Here's an example:

Love Interest's Thumb:	50
Fingers:	+35
TOTAL:	85

Now out of these totals you make a fraction, dividing your thumb and finger total by theirs: It looks like this:

Your Thumb/Finger Total:	80
Their Thumb/Finger Total:	85
THE MULTIPLE:	80 divided by 85 = .94

Third: Multiply Score A by the Multiple

Score A:	63
Multiple of	.94
SCORE B	59.22

Fourth: Subtract Score B from Score A to arrive at your Compatibility Quotient. In this case we would have:

$$63 \text{ minus } 59.22 = +3.78$$

Please note that in this example the average of the four comparative percentages (hand shape, Lines of Life, Head and Heart), or score A, is reduced by the thumb/finger fraction (your thumb total divided by your partner's thumb's total) which is called the Multiple. The product of the Multiple times Score A gives Score B. In this instance the Score B (59.22) is less than Score A (63), yielding a Compatibility Quotient (A minus B) of (+3.78). While I do think this is a possible match for the person making the comparison, it is clear that the love interest is a stronger person. The Compatibility Quotient (+3.78) is reasonably good. Thus +3.78 figure is something to note carefully, for the partner wanting to control the relationship will be an issue. The compatibility number is close enough to make it a go-for-it situation, if a strong partner is desired and there is good communication.

Let's look at another example. Let's say your lover's thumb/finger score total was 70 and we divide this into your score of 80. Seventy divided by 80 yields the multiple 1.14. Now there will be a real difference if Score A (overall compatibility of first four characteristics) is also 63: 1.14 times 63 = 71.99. Subtracting 71.99 from 63 gives a Compatibility Quotient of almost negative nine (−9). Are you in charge of this relationship? I should say so! The negative score of this individual puts too much power on your side. You have a lot of control and may not be challenged by this person.

To help you understand how to evaluate the postive and negative number shift in this process, the following scale with comments is provided. Remember, these numbers relate to the shift in Score A, which is multiplied by the Multiple and then reduced or increased by Score B. Don't panic over this math. You are doing less-than-seventh-grade work and it has a proven accuracy in helping you handicap a relationship. Try it; you'll see. Start with your friends. You'll soon catch on and become an old pro at this, and be able to *see* the difference without the math. With this measuring method in mind you'll instantly see things differently.

The key is to remember that a negative number for your Compatibility Quotient means this person is not as strong in this evaluation format as you are. A positive score means this person is stronger than you are on this scale. Do you like a challenge or do you want to be the boss? Either way, the numbers will tell you what you need to know.

Compare the results of your Compatibility Quotient to my evaluations below.

Scores of −15 to −10: Do you like doormats? You are too powerful for a real exchange of equals. Check your motivation for keeping such a mismatch going.

Scores −9 to −5: You are nearly overpowering your partner. Develop patience and listening skills.

Scores −4 to 0: A good match; you have a balanced mix of involvement. Your skills and personality can lead the way.

Score +01 to +05: You are challenged by your partner, but the exchange is stimulating and you can grow. Stretch yourself.

Scores +06 to +10: Your partner is much stronger, but even the lion can have a thorn in its paw. You must work hard, but it may be worth it if the chemistry is right.

Scores +11 to +15: Watch out! You are outgunned by your partner, who will dominate your tastes and desires. When was the last time *you* chose the movie? Buy a parachute.

Please explore your own way of working with these numbers. You will gain confidence and accuracy in your system. These general score levels have worked for me. Good luck!

PART ✣ TWO

THE FINE TUNING

This second half of Romance on Your Hands *will deal with minor lines on the hand, those fine-tuning points that can have important implications in understanding how a person may function in a relationship. While not as important as the major lines and hand characteristics of Part One, these lines are like the spice in the stew, the dressing on the salad, the topping on your favorite yogurt.*

Study these lines with an eye toward what they add to or detract from the basic character and compatibility principles outlined already. I'll make suggestions as to how these lines work in different pairing situations. Add these insights to your growing compatibility picture with a certain someone, or just to augment your own self-awareness and understanding of your interpersonal needs.

7

THE LINE
of FATE

The Line of Fate might more aptly be called the Line of Character and Career. Even in the writings of Saint-Germain in the nineteenth century, this line was not considered one of deterministic destiny, but of "life work," implying that choice as well as the wheel of fortune are active in shaping a person's life.

To the modern palmist, the Fate Line reveals a synthesis of information about how a person's character functions in the give-and-take with the Plain of Mars. Rather then being an indication of the blind twists of circumstance, the line emerges from these trials in the heat (Mars) of life to reveal the strength of personal independence and career drive, and provides a gauge of one's ability to adapt to change and to cope with the challenge of the environment. In this instance, the environment is the fate, the given—the hometown, the family, the height, weight, and ailments. The will and its choices, which the line measures, provide ways for the individual to cope with these given ingredients.

What makes this line unique is its perpendicular flow in relation to other lines. It rises from the base of the hand, travels vertically up the Plain of Mars, and crosses both the Line of Head and Line of Heart (and sometimes the Line of Mercury). It is thus a line of synthesis and cross-communication ending up under the Finger of Saturn, showing solid character and a successful career. Sometimes the line will angle toward Jupiter in its termination, indicating a natural ability to lead and direct.

The key symbolism to understand in evaluating the Line of Fate is that it divides the hand vertically: the rational side is Saturn, Jupiter, and Rhea (middle finger, index finger, and thumb); the imaginative side is Apollo, Mercury, and Luna (ring finger, little finger, outer palm of the hand).

The Line's central position in the hand is not its only unique feature. It is also the first line studied so far to have an abstract meaning, "fate" being less concretely defined than "life," "head," or "heart." The line can symbolize how the many attributes of the hand are brought together in a blend to form a greater whole. It can be seen as a "plumb line" in the center of the hand which can quickly tell you the "bent" of a person's character. Let's now look at the line in a progressive way, examining its meaning from the most basic consideration—the depth and texture of the line—to the more complicated large patterns that affect success and compatibility.

First, look at the texture of the Line of Fate. A nice *deep continuous line* shows that the ability to cope with reality is strong, that the incentive to make a career is strong, and the drive to succeed has a vital, motivating force.

If the line is splintered, feathered, frayed, or islanded, the energies which go into centering the personality are divided and weakened. The person is often at odds with himself and the thrust of the character is diffused and lacks focus. Such an individual may miss opportunities, expend energy unwisely, or respond too slowly or too hysterically to input. Moodiness or other psychological impairments may also be problems.

The *origin* of the line *near the base of the hand* indicates that the individual came to an understanding of the nature of his personality at an early age. These are people who even in preschool seemed to have set characters and to be definitely going in a certain direction.

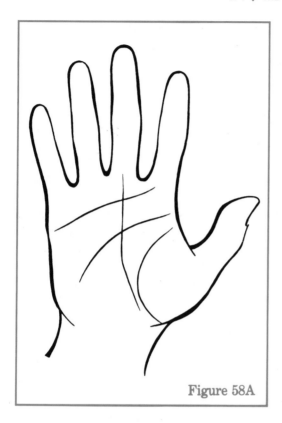

Figure 58A

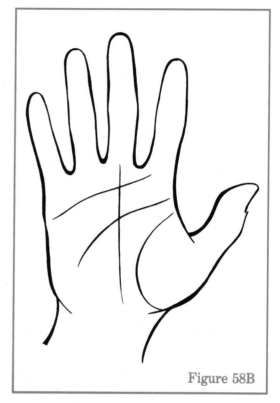

Figure 58B

If the line is centered (figure 58A), the individual is a middle-of-the-road person, balancing his personality between reason and imagination, among family, the neighborhood, and the outside influence of school and friends. These individuals are very good at politicking, ingratiating themselves, and ending up on top. They are usually sophisticated or streetwise due to early experiences and can be successful in their careers. Personalities formed when young, however, may not be very flexible, so other aspects of the hand (thumb and Head Line, for example) should be checked for openness and creativity.

When the line forms on the far right (figure 58B) near the Line of Life, the influence of the family must be considered in all interactions with this individual.

The traditions of the home, the career options his family has consistently chosen over the years, will all play a very vital part in the career and character of this person. Any successful relationship with such an individual requires the ability to deal with his heavy emphasis on tradition, even family approval.

If the Line of Fate starts left, or deep in Luna or Neptune (figure 58C), the individual is more a product of his or her own imagination—or of the influence of people outside the family. These people may feel like aliens in their home environment and turn to reading or movies or other sources for role models as a way to shape their view of themselves and how they wish to evolve. Teachers, coaches, the parents of friends, the friends themselves, may well have a great effect on their life. The key to their personalities is their intense feeling of being different and the role that the powers of Luna (imagination) and Neptune (archetypal consciousness) play in the shaping of the persona. These people will often take the road less traveled and expect their spouses to follow suit.

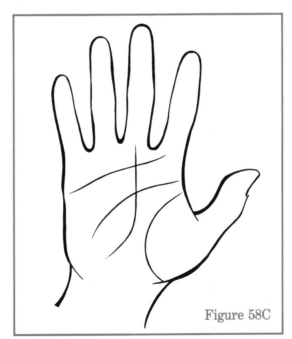

Figure 58C

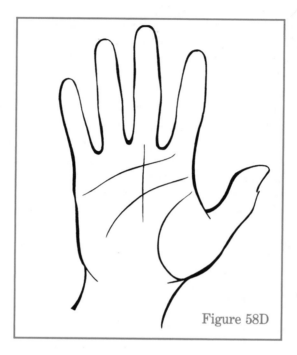

Figure 58D

If the Line of Fate is branched at the beginning, it indicates that the individual draws from the imaginative and the traditional forces that shape the growth of character and career.

When the Line of Fate starts in the middle of the palm under the Line of Head (figure 58D), it indicates that the identity and character of the individual come into focus during the period after college. The best way to judge timing in this situation is to consider the Head Line's intersection with the Line of Fate to represent about age thirty. To gauge the beginning of a Fate line, use this scale and read the line as you would a road map. The example in Figure 58D shows a Fate line which starts at about age twenty-four, meaning that this is the age where real "individuation" (to quote Jung) begins. Ask about what happened at that age and chances are you'll get an earful.

As we will see in later chapters the same "center principle" applies to the meaning of other minor lines originating in this middle position. *If the line* (figure 58E) *originates from the Life Line side*, it indicates a more traditional development. *Should the line* (figure 58F) *rise on the Luna side*, the imaginative and external influences predominate.

All individuals with the Fate Line starting midpalm are people who have discovered who they are after going through their teens and early twenties. They are often in the group who didn't know in high school or early college exactly what it was that they wanted. These folks can be excellent in relationships. They are willing to work for a mutually defined relationship, knowing that it is a process that takes time and effort and is characterized by periods of both ambiguity and breakthrough.

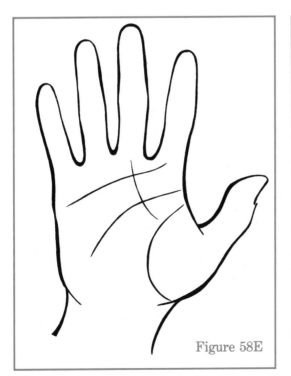

Figure 58E

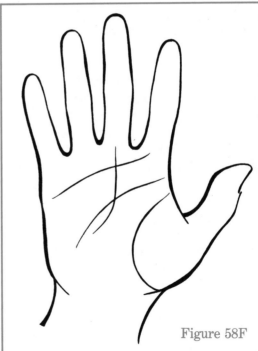

Figure 58F

When the Fate Line originates near the Line of Heart (figure 58G), it indicates that at a midlife crisis the individual will really make his or her personal and career breakthrough. This midlife energy brings together the elements of success and will mean fulfillment to people who have often felt held back in their attempts to realize the potential of their talents. These people are commonly termed "late bloomers." The way that late blooming manifests itself depends on the position of the origin of the line. The "center principle" again prevails: the Apollo side is creativity and imagination (figure 58H), the Jupiter side conventional wisdom and family tradition (figure 58I). The central-spot of origin is a combination of the two.

These late bloomers are marvelous, for they have lived life a long time before hitting their true stride. They know the frustration of not knowing exactly when or how circumstances were going to give them a shot at success. Thus these individuals are going to be very understanding about the simple turns of fate that make life turn out differently from our high school expectations and college plans. One late bloomer told me, "Success came so late, it doesn't matter anymore. I know I'm a man without it."

Take a tip from an old, experienced palm reader: never be fooled by present circumstance. I have seen the mighty fall and the lowly rise many a time. What you see before you at present is exactly that. It can all change, and one of the clues to perceiving the direction of this next spin of the wheel are the lines on the hand. Once I worked for a young broker who speculated in commodities. He'd bought a big house and threw Gatsby-style parties. A giant break in his Fate Line told me to expect a fall. And it happened: he was caught in a scam that cost him everything. A young woman seeing this on his Fate Line would think twice about getting seriously involved with him.

Breaks in the Fate Line are very important (figure 59A). *Breaks* show a modification or change in the development of the career and character. They may well represent a challenge that had to be met, but which was such an experience that the fabric of the individual's personality was rent somewhat, enlarged, or changed.

The most common shift is that *the line moves to the Luna side of the palm* a sixteenth of an inch or more. The break at the Line of Head (point #1 in figure 59A) means that as a result of a challenge this person had to loosen up and make imaginative and creative changes in his life. One often sees this in individuals who

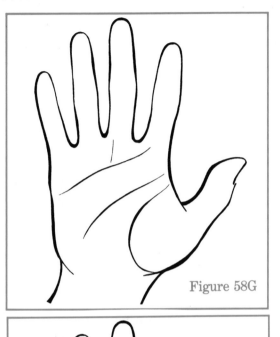

Figure 58G

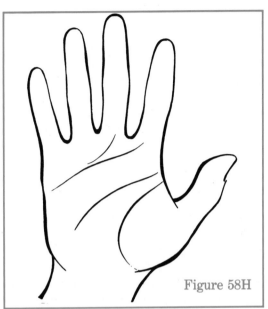

Figure 58H

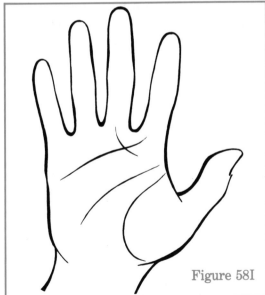

Figure 58I

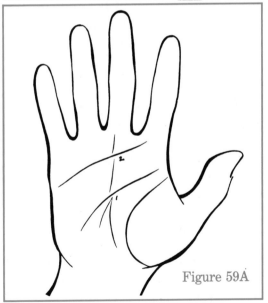

Figure 59A

are so extremely authoritative that one knows they will not be humanly lovable until they loosen up, get the shiny paint off their phony gleaming teeth, get off that high horse and join the rest of the human race.

Similarly, *when the shift is toward the thumb*, it indicates a new level of self-discipline, an ability to deal with authority, or a new wisdom that sees some type of conformity as good (like abstaining from drugs, booze, and gambling). A shift toward the thumb is demonstrated when the prodigal son comes to his senses, or the wanton woman becomes the saint.

When a branch comes and joins the Line of Fate (figure 59B, line 1), it indicates the type of influence that affects the person. If the merger of the lines is smooth, the outside influence was helpful; if it appears that the branch line and the Fate Line collide and fail to merge as one line, it suggests that the event was disruptive—though possibly still productive in the long run. The nature of the input from the branch line needs to be analyzed in terms of where it originates—left, center, or right—to know more about the particulars of the event.

Often branch lines originate in deep Neptune, causing disruption in the Fate Line (figure 59B, point 2). This break can indicate a meeting with a fantasy-come-true romantic lover. Young women and men often dream of perfect lovers and passionately seek them. Often only the nightmare wakes them up. The break in the fate line indicates the jolt.

The way that the Line of Fate ends gives a big glue to the final direction of the individual's career. *When the line ends under the Finger of Jupiter* (figure 60A), look for management, consulting, or politics to show up in the career scope. These people work hard, are good at supervising, and get results.

When the Line of Fate ends under the Finger of Apollo (figure 60B), the refined arts, literature, drama, motion pictures, music, commercials, arts, design, architecture, writing, and journalism are all possible career areas. These individuals will be a little more high-strung and more conscious of their lifestyle as well as their personal environment. This feature is also indicative of self-employed free-lancers who create their own jobs, especially in marketing and public relations.

When the line ends directly under Saturn (figure 60C), the ability to measure, weigh, and probe is very strong. This individual's personality is solid and oriented toward many concrete aptitudes. *If the line touches the base of the middle finger,* it is a sign of great strength in character with an excellent sense of money.

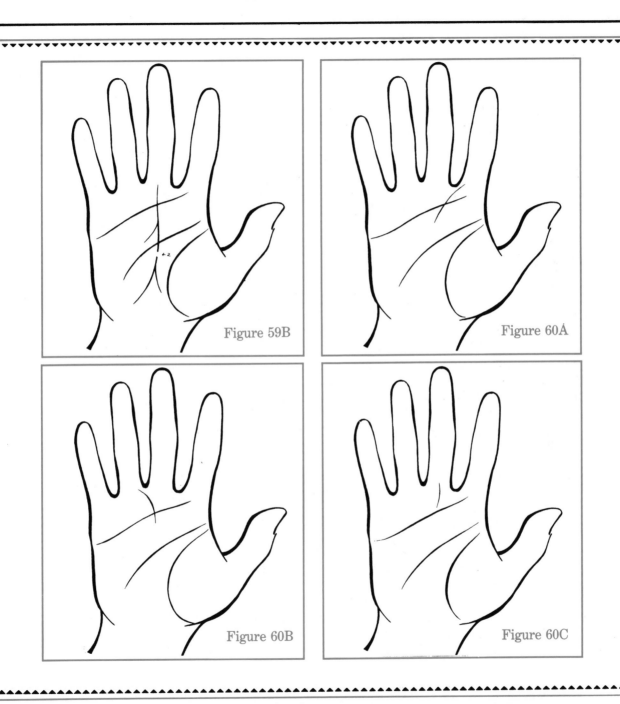

Figure 59B

Figure 60A

Figure 60B

Figure 60C

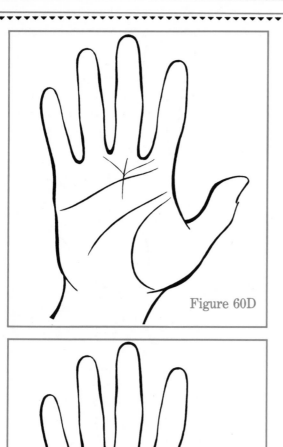

Figure 60D

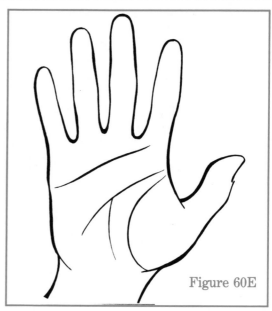

Figure 60E

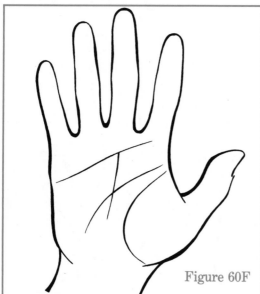

Figure 60F

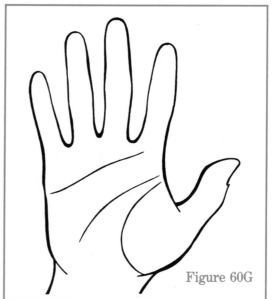

Figure 60G

When the line splits at the end (figure 60D), it means that the individual offers a rare combination of many diverse skills. These multitalented people can "do it all" and often do—arts, management, and other data-intense fields. They are the ultimate jugglers. In relationships, these individuals will be able to fit in with lots of different types of people. They're usually found to be extremely popular, because they can interact with so many different people on so many different levels.

When the line seems to end at the Line of Head (figure 60E), it is a sign that this person's mental outlook is very strong, and that he will attempt to control his life's direction with clear mental decisions. Whether these decisions will bear success can be determined by the quality of the Line of Apollo, which we will examine in more detail shortly. If the Line of Apollo is well developed, this person's decisive attitude will work in almost any situation. These people may be hard to deal with in relationships, because they demand much mental discipline in themselves. They're the ones who'll regularly say, "I did it this way; you should too."

When the line ends in the Heart Line (figure 60F), the direction of this person's life is being governed by emotional needs. It doesn't matter what all the facts can say, a proposition or situation must "feel" right. This contributes to an intuitive approach to all matters of life that often serves the individual's needs wonderfully. Sometimes, though, there is a potential hazard of irrational fears or emotional fixations creeping in, which can make dealing with such an individual quite an ordeal. Look to the Line of Apollo for an indication of the success of this emotional approach. A strong Line of Apollo says the intuitive attitude is working, whereas the weaker or absent Line of Apollo can spell trouble in emotional areas. Either way, this line configuration suggests that this person is highly volatile in relationships. There is a lot more instinct than reason operating in this person's makeup.

What if there is *no Fate Line?* (figure 60G) Don't panic! Contrary to Saint-Germain's belief that the absence of the line meant an "eventless life," it more accurately indicates that the individual is open to lots of different approaches and possibilities. It is a sign of one who is young at heart, carefree, and delightfully spontaneous. This is sometimes found on the hands of an individual who may feel overshadowed by a parent or sibling. I once had a very successful client who had no Fate Line. It turned out that the man's father consistently outshone him, at least in my client's eyes. Evidently, inferiority is in the eyes of the beholder.

Some palmistry books are very pessimistic about hands with no Fate Line. Comments can vary from "has trouble finding a place in life" to "destined to a life without achievement." I find this simply not true. The absence of a Fate Line can occur in individuals who are common laborers or whose choices in life have been dictated by others. However, many who lack this line are marvelously successful, often endearingly childlike, and capable of creating a charmed existence at any level of society.

In relationships, those who have no Fate Line are lots of fun, but these folks can be alarmingly like Peter Pan and Tinkerbell. For a while joining them in their passionate, emotional romps under the stars will bring hours of joy. But once issues of responsibility come into play, when it is so important to develop trust, the relationship may fall apart. And if you can't trust someone to share in the day-to-day responsibilities of the material world, no amount of fun or frolic can make up for the rough ride ahead. Nevertheless, if you're looking for someone who is spontaneous, outgoing, and remarkably versatile, here is a breath of fresh air. Trust your personal judgment and limits of tolerance when encountering this one!

When lines of influence (figure 61A) *cross the Line of Life and also cross the Line of Fate*, the individual is experiencing some interference from family or others close to him or her. Sometimes these influence lines are very intense and can be extremely telling even on first encounters. The key is to realize that the person you've just met has a large amount of emotional baggage to work through in dealings with family or close friends. I have seen over and over how these lines are cold evidence of meddling families, found frequently on the hands of women who go from a meddling family to a harsh husband, just to keep up the rhythm of abuse. One such woman finally woke up one day, got divorced, and started an independent life of her own.

Finally, consider this timing map (figure 61B) as a way to gauge timing on the Line of Fate. Although the ratios and proportions of these age estimations are correct, they need to be adjusted to the particular hand you are reading. Some people will experience things a little sooner, others a little later. After asking a few questions and getting a feel for the sequence of events in a person's life, you will be able to improve in accuracy.

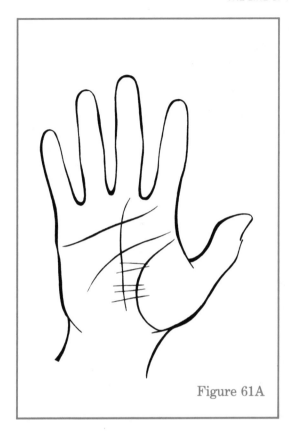

Figure 61A

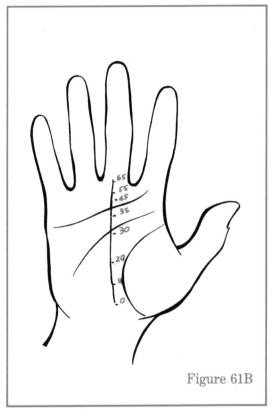

Figure 61B

Now ponder carefully the many different aspects of the Line of Fate, using your new knowledge. It is a very important line, whose contour and shape can reveal a multitude of things about an individual's character and career. The nature of his staying power, the timing of his large life changes, the greatest influences on his personal and financial developments, all are laid out in subtle symbolism. Study here will pay off handsomely when you are evaluating someone as a prospect in a relationship.

8

THE LINE
of APOLLO

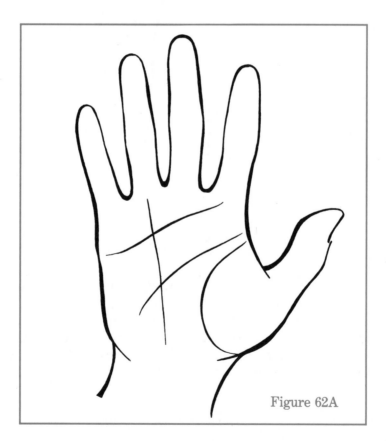

Figure 62A

THE "SUN-CESS" LINE

The Line of Apollo (figure 62A) is a difficult line to define. Palmists for centuries have swapped ideas about its real meaning. Apollo is the god who pulled the sun around heaven behind his golden chariot, and it is in the shining glory of this Sun god that man can find a gleam of success. "Make hay while the sun shines" is an old phrase that celebrates the symbol of the sun as an opportunity to make prosperity happen. The "sun" could be the literal sun, the "hay" could mean literal hay. Or the sun could symbolize a streak of luck at your job, which makes you symbolic hay—money! Similarly, consider two approaches to the Line of Apollo that have kept palmists busy for eons: Does the line represent success as the light of fame shining through a talent or skill? Or, as the second point of view asks, does the line represent success in terms of making money? The two are not necessarily the same. All rich men are not famous and all famous men are not rich. So when you see a nice Sun Line on your lover's palm, does that mean fame, money, both, or what? Read on and see!

Before we examine the particular paths this line takes on the hand and how it relates to romance, let's take a good look at some of the various meanings it has been given. First, I must mention that I have seen people with enormous wealth and power without a Sun Line. Yet I have never seen a movie star of socialite without one.

How can people make money and *not* have the Sun Line? It became very obvious to me on an occasion when I was reading palms as the fashionable "occult entertainment" at a huge aircraft company's top executive awards banquet. Imagine all these powerful chief executives with their glamorous ladies sitting at round tables in the ballroom of a lavish hotel. Most of these very successful men did not have Lines of Sun, but did have strong Lines of Fate. Why did this pattern occur in so many of the hands? As it turned out, this particular aircraft company was a defense contractor and had just built a top-secret bomber. It was a highly classified and secret operation. Thus, the Line of Sun was muted on so many of their hands. These men kept low profiles.

This experience, along with other "hands-on" research, convinced me that wealth and responsibility can occur without a Sun Line. What, then, does this line mean?

First of all, let's consider the Sun Line, or the Line of Apollo, as a parallel or sister line to the Line of Fate. The Fate Line is ruled by Saturn, the strongest taskmaster in the pantheon of Greek and Roman gods. Saturn stands for the material world. At one time Saturn was thought to be the outer limit of the solar system. As a god, Saturn was the master of measurable reality, the lord of karma, the judge of results, the definer of limits. It is because it is governed by these qualities that the Line of Fate expresses the two hard nuggets by which we define ourselves in our environment—character and career.

Yet the god Apollo was also powerful—the ruler of charisma, style, healing, and the prophetic voice. Apollo was the eloquent god of talent and the trigger or stimulus for aesthetics. Thus the Line of Apollo, the Line of Sun, has often been called the "Line of Brilliance." Others have called it the "Line of Reputation," while still others term it the "Line of Personal Image." And these factors certainly play a vital part in shaping romance.

The following general points will make the Line of Sun easier to interpret. As Apollo was also known as the god of music, you might think of these eight rules as an octave of information. When you see a Line of Sun on a hand one or more of these eight points will be true.

1 ♥ The Line of Sun can add glory and eloquence to the Fate Line.
2 ♥ It indicates popularity or fame in whatever social milieu the individual enjoys.
3 ♥ Artistic or creative talent is usually present.
4 ♥ Intellectual refinement is often present.
5 ♥ Lifestyle is very important.
6 ♥ Sense of self will be more romantic and visionary.
7 ♥ The Apollonian prowess at prophecy makes this person highly intuitive.
8 ♥ The length and shape of the finger type (realistic, receptive, active, analytical) will influence the way the qualities of Apollo manifest themselves. For example, on a realistic hand a well-defined Sun Line could be read as someone who integrates realism and art, such as a highly sought-after foreign sports car mechanic. For some people this profession is high art!

Most of these points are clearly facets that we would find important in a lover. Romance means style, class, refinement. The degree of refinement will be read

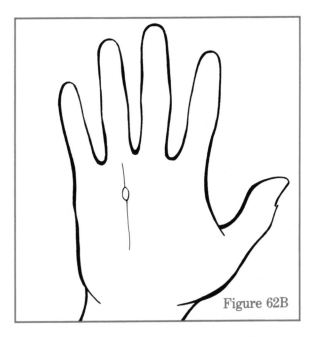

Figure 62B

through clues in the pages that follow. Let's get to the line itself. Remember basic palmistry principles—the better shaped, the deeper and fuller the line, the greater the positive effect. The *deep Line of Sun* is a wonderful sight to see on a hand. It gives the full depth and brilliance of Apollo to the individual. There is an extra glow to these people. We want to love them! They stand out, their talents seem grander. They have a bit of what astrologers call the Leo "aura" to them. They dazzle us.

When the line is irregular, feathered, frayed, or otherwise distorted, there is a direct effect on the manifestation of talent. The individual may be inconsistent, lack follow-through, have ego problems, or suffer setbacks in social status. Some books claim that an *island on this line* (figure 62B) means scandal. I have not found this to be so. An island means a point of divided concerns, a setback because the focus of energies has gone askew. "Scandal" doesn't get to the heart of the problem. When an island splits the concentration, only sloppy results can occur. Try to watch TV and talk on the phone at the same time and you'll experience the way that islands can bring screw-ups.

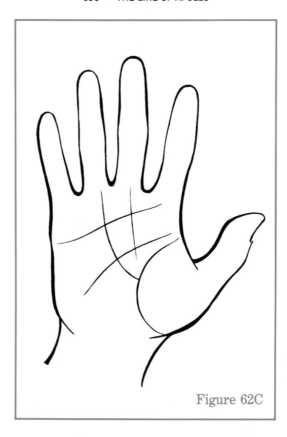

Figure 62C

The long Line of Sun (figure 62A) is a sign of long-developed talent with a balance of support from friends and family. *When the line swings over toward or touches the Line of Life* (figure 62C), the individual owes an early success to the help and influence of another who is either in the immediate or extended family. Know when you see this sign that you court the person and marry the family.

When the Line of Sun originates in either of the Mounts of Luna or Neptune, (figure 62D), the person gains respect and reputation through an excellent imagination that is supported by a mentor or someone outside the family circle. This can

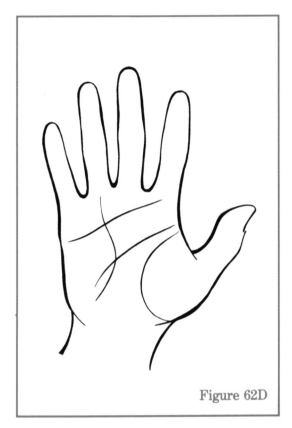

Figure 62D

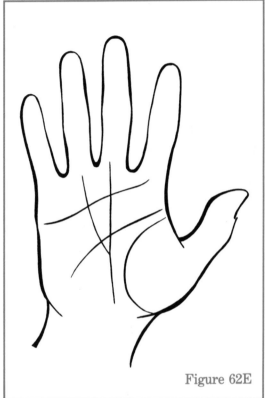

Figure 62E

be a teacher, a talent scout, or simply someone from outside who champions this individual's talents. It might be the counselor who encouraged the student to apply for a scholarship or the clothing manufacturer who allowed the apprentice to have a chance at doing the design work. This type is independent in love.

When the line originates from the Line of Fate (figure 62E), this person will have a natural flow of good reputation during the evolution of his or her career. This is a strong mark; it assures both the money and status that a talented individual deserves. These folks may love their career most of all.

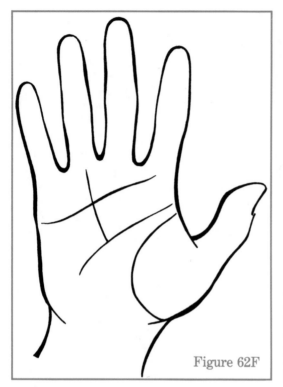

Figure 62F

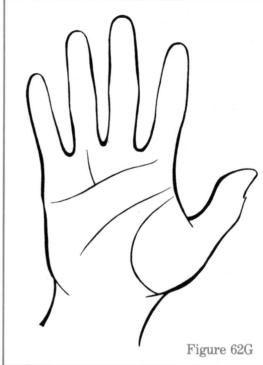

Figure 62G

When the line originates from the Head Line (figure 62F), the individual is brilliant and has numerous talents. The mental instincts are naturally subtle and refined. This person will have carefully sculpted acquired tastes which are inspired by a unique aesthetic. In this case, style is of the essence. By the time the individual is in his or her mid-thirties, these traits should be fully operative and he or she may perhaps be well known, or at least a prominent reputation will be in the making. In love these people can be headstrong.

When the line originates from the Line of Heart (figure 62G), you'll know that you have discovered a very passionate personality and someone who is most appreciative of the arts. These people often come into their glory in their forties or later. Such passion, so long in blossoming, is much to be savored.

Classical palmists claim that *if three lines come up from the Heart Line onto the Mount of Apollo* (figure 63A), it is a sign of immense luck arising from that person's versatility. More than three lines is considered unlucky in that the talents are being dissipated and the energies spread too thin. It has been my observation that too many lines on the Mount of Apollo fall on the hands of those who have little control of their talent, and unfortunately, little success. These individuals can be versatile in love, and they like changes of pace.

If the line swerves to the Mount of Saturn (figure 63B), all happiness, fame, reputation, and success will result from serious study and leadership. The individual has had to bear up under much pressure from real tests. One might describe them

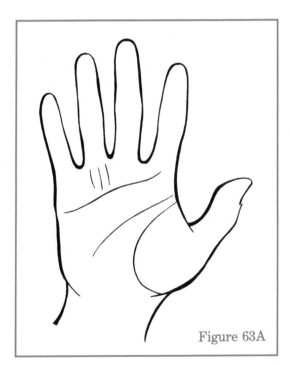

Figure 63A

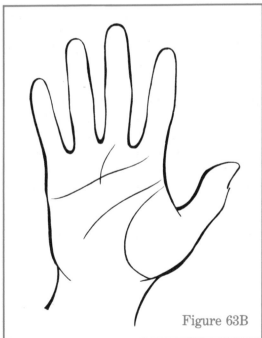

Figure 63B

as "tests of fire"—arduous rigors that eventually pay off in substantial ways. Also, this person has true brilliance and correspondingly will take art and romance very seriously. You must perform to their standards to be appreciated.

When the line of Sun ends directly under Apollo (figure 63C), the brilliance is of an aesthetic purity. The ability to see life in grand romantic terms is easily expressed. This person is quick and natural in his or her sense of style, and in how things hit the eyes and ears. From fashion to politics, this guy or gal is a major crowd pleaser.

When the Line swerves to the Mount of Mercury (figure 63D), the brilliance is in business or communication. These folks are quick to see how a dollar is made, and are whiz kids at analyzing the market. They're excellent communicators and usually find themselves in professions that are media- or communications-related. They know how to talk your socks off. And when it comes to romance, these men and women make fascinating lovers with their constant expression of feelings and ideas.

All in all the Line of Sun is an important line to find on lovers. Its presence indicates a stylistic hue to their romantic qualities, which must be coupled with the major signals of the Heart Line. A straight and mentally controlled Heart Line and a strong Line of Sun are indicative of a very stylized person that some would find cold, others would say reserved with flair. Conversely, if the Heart Line is curved and passionate, the individual would communicate this passion with fitting taste.

The presence of a strong Line of Sun is always a sign of someone who can socialize within a peer group. Whether she's Queen of the bowling alley or he's King of Wall Street, the Apollonian strain is a mark of being able to move with grace in groups.

Remember, this is a minor line. It is not as easy to account for a person's romantic or personal attributes just on this line. Rather, you must look on this line as a powerful spice that can effectively sharpen or blunt other qualities in the hand. Take your time, make mental notes of the Line of Sun on the hands you examine, and soon you'll be able to spot the subtle and remarkable ways Apollo can enhance life and romance.

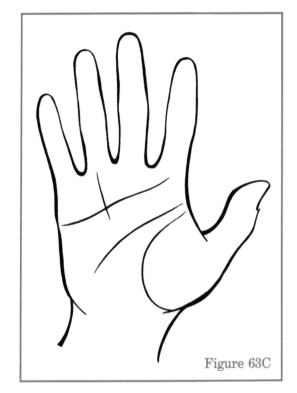

Figure 63C

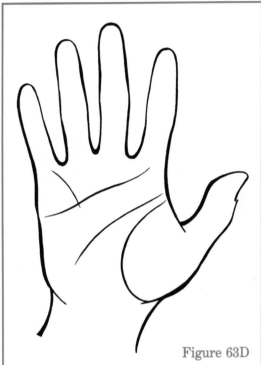

Figure 63D

9

THE LINES
of
MARRIAGE

T he Lines of Marriage. The very sound of these words can send thoughts flying to rapturous heights as one romantically contemplates a deep and lasting love. Young ladies and gents spend many formative days and nights dreaming about the day when they will walk down the aisle with their Prince or Princess Charming. The New Age idea of "soul mates," of pairing with the soul of someone one has known in "past lives," has only heightened the interest in the many concepts related to loving and coupling. Add to this latest craze the time-honored Western theme of preordained lovers ("it was meant to be") and the plot thickens. What is your destiny? Will you find "true love" and marriage. What can palmistry tell you about what is "meant to be" in your love life?

There is a great deal of hype—exaggerated claims—that surrounds most readings of the Lines of Marriage. The public's chronic obsession with love has created an even greater number of old wives' tales about the Lines of Marriage. These are superstitions based on the whims of the public and have no inherent logic. So it is necessary for me to throw a few grains of reality into this discussion. The truth is that no lines on the hand get as much attention, scrutiny, pondering, wishing, and hoping than those that are said to predict a long and fruitful marriage. Still, no part of palmistry is more subject to vagaries, misinterpretations, and outright inaccuracies than the part that attempts to deal with lasting unions between humans. It seems that many have overlooked common sense as an important "sixth sense" when reading the precious, subtle truths in the Lines of Marriage. And, in the words of Samuel Taylor Coleridge, "Common sense in an uncommon degree is what the world calls wisdom." So let's be wise when we explore these lines.

The ancient Hindus had wisdom when they, first in the recorded history of palmreading, wrote of these Lines of Marriage. We should recall that their perspective was from a time when all marriages were arranged, a practice that has not completely ended even in our time. The intent of the Hindu writings was to gauge the aptitude toward marriage of the individual, and to assess the energies of the two candidates involved.

In the West, the whole world of sex and marriage was turned upside down by a revolution of consciousness when medieval Western culture got wind of the romantic concept of love. Imagine thinking that people pick their own spouses! And then, after the acknowledgment of romance as a determination in the matrimonial choice, suddenly the idea that it was possible to change your mind about a partner began to gain slow but steady recognition. Gradually, divorce became the rule rather than the exception. In the twentieth century, many people do not get married for life. They go through a form of "serial monogamy," marrying more than once or even twice. Further contributing factors in this revolution have included the sexual liberation brought on by the birth-control pill, the women's movement, and the expansion of women's rights. These dramatic changes have occurred in a relatively short period of time.

This historical background brings us to the crisis in palmistry today. How can the hand begin to cope with such an onslaught of sudden change? To answer the question succinctly—it can't. In this day of such wide-ranging ideas and lifestyles, from the wildly experimental to the very conservative, to look for absolute answers in the Lines of Marriage in the hands is to fail to wake up and smell the coffee. Clearly, the meaning of these lines must be rethought!

What the Lines of Marriage can do is shed special light on the attitudes and psychology of an individual as they relate to marriage. Insights not available in other lines can be garnered here, as well as the unveiling of certain feelings kept secret. Let me warn of a common problem that can occur. As a specialist, I tend to have a knack for calling the relationships shown in these lines with impressive specificity—that is, most of the time. Regularly, it is possible to make predictions about marriage and kids with great accuracy. Rumors fly through a party or a clique of friends seeking private readings, that purport of a seer who has no equal. Then with other individuals and other circumstances, interpreting the same lines in the same way, the readings will fall flat-footed wrong. Carol White, a wonderful palmist, has commented that these marriage lines are so unpredictable that they are almost a liability to use.

Having addressed my professional ethics with these honest, forthright warnings, let's turn our attention to the topic at hand. It is worthwhile to be aware that the naming of these lines as marriage lines is still a matter of dispute for many modern palmists. They are most often referred to as Lines of Union, Lines of Affection, or simply Lines of Love. Personally, I view and sometimes speak of each line as a "mark of the heart's commitment." They mark relationships that have made permanent and indelible inroads into the deepest affections, and may or may not have anything to do with marriage. One might represent the lover who went to war and never returned, another a special person who was taken away by a tragic accident. One Line of Marriage might have been a mere infatuation—that love you had that summer you were in Europe studying. How about that neighbor down the hall when you moved into your first apartment? There are countless emotional environments where deep love can happen and not necessarily lead to marriage. And yet, the hand honors that most sincere relationship with a line to denote its effect on you. Remember, marriage can be love or it can be a contract, a legal agreement. You must decide what kind of relationship you're in. You must decide what kind you want and you must be careful.

The evolution of the soul through its quest for love and self-awareness is a key theme in modern attempts to find meaning in a world that often seems absurd. There are five areas on the hand that yield information about the heart's commitment—or lack of it. This topography of relationship is a varied and interlocking terrain. Approach this study with intuition, common sense, and notions of "what you see might be what you get," or "what you see might be what you hoped for, but getting it will be hard work" or even a grain of "what you see may not be there at all."

I have found that the real learning to be reaped from reading the Lines of Marriage can be priceless. If these lines inspire you to a deeper contemplation about the meaning of love in your life, then the lines have served a high purpose. And if your prediction of a marriage comes true, then you will feel the elation of having been accurate!

The five areas where treasure chests of information for love and marriage lines can be found are:

1. ♥ On the Mount of Mercury (under the little finger).
2. ♥ On the area across the Mount of Nepture to the Line of Fate (percussion side of hand).
3. ♥ Lines inside the Inner Line of Life on the Mount of Venus (base of thumb).
4. ♥ The condition of the "Ring of Family" on the thumb.
5. ♥ Special marks and lines that denote very special conditions of circumstances.

Each of these areas has a special meaning and interfaces often with the lines on other parts of the hand. Each part must be seen in the larger webbing of the whole.

LINES ON THE MOUNT OF MERCURY

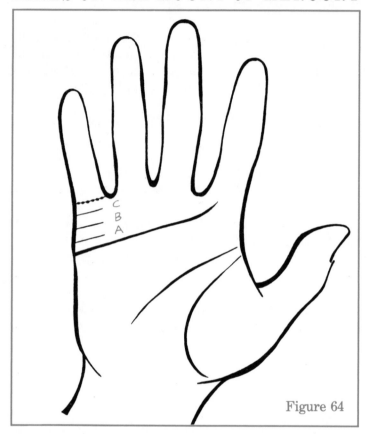

Figure 64

The Mount of Mercury, *between the Line of Heart and the joint of the little finger's third phalange* is an area where traditionalists will search for the "Lines of Union," or as I prefer to call them, the "Lines of Affection" (figure 64). Lines on this mount should be examined carefully for both number and depth. For years palmists have pointed out that the Mount of Mercury is a "mental mount." Hence, the lines one finds there may not represent the nature of the marriages themselves, but the mental attitude of the subject to marriage.

As a basic ground rule, I employ the idea that the greatest resource for a thriving relationship is communication. That is exactly what the Mount of Mercury is all about: communication, mental compatability, inner archetypes. Without mutual confidence and honest expression, any relationship is destined to be a dud. The heart may be passionate, the mind sharp, the life dynamic, but without the ability to share all that with another, or a weakness in this zone, a combination is created that spells something similar to what the Hermit Card in Tarot represents—an ultimately sad loner—or worse. Take the analogy of the grand scheme to erect the Tower of Babel. All participating had the best of intentions, yet the building never came to fruition because of poor communication. The most intimate form of expression exists within relationships, and among the many influences in the palm it is Mercury and Cupid who carry the love notes of Venus.

To determine the *timing* of a relationship when looking at the Lines of Affection, check *the distance from the Heart Line at the base of the Mount of Mercury to the beginning of the little finger* (see figure 64). The earliest ages (line A) are those near the Heart Line and grow progressively older right up to the finger joint. Generally, you can allow fifteen years for every quarter inch or so, progressing fifteen, thirty (line B), forty-five (line C). This will enable you to approximate the age of the individual at the time of the relationship—sometimes with sharp accuracy. This can be confirmed with even more certainty when relationship lines appear in two different areas of the palm with similar chronology. You might detect a love affair at age thirty on the Mount of Mercury, and observe a mark for spiritual connection on the Mount of Luna, also at the age of thirty. Both areas speak of the same relationship, and in noting both you'll be allowed much greater confidence in the validity of this relationship. We'll discuss the comparison of the timing of relationships in further detail once we have finished our trek through Mercury.

The thickness and length of the lines on the Mount of Mercury are the keys that unlock and reveal how significant the particular relationship is to the individual (figure 65). Light lines (see lines A & B) show heavy flirtations or affairs. A deep line, whether short or long, that extends onto the surface of the mount represents a serious relationship. This can be either a marriage or a union that has many of the same aspects as marriage; a steady sex life, living together or sleeping over a lot, and also traveling together.

It is not uncommon to find a hand with *one deep line* (figure 65, line C) *and a couple of lighter lines* (A & B). This pattern depicts an individual who has had a couple of semiserious relationships before settling down in a marriage or a long-term commitment. Regularly, there will have been a sweetheart, perhaps a college romance, that initiated the individual into the passions of romance.

Individuals with only one long Line of Marriage (C) on their hands or one short but deep line (D) are usually very monogamous. This is a man or woman who is often found to be married to the very same love interest who first tugged at his or her heartstrings in the blush of youth. If there is a second marriage, this individual will be as faithful to the second partner as to the first. *Should the line be strong but break and have a sister line running next to it* (figure 65, line E), you'll detect a relationship that has grown distant. The two parties in this relationship may live together or apart, but they do maintain a form of contact and have come to a partial resolution—separate bedrooms perhaps. At other times, the individual has an inflexible attitude that divorce is wrong, and the marriage hangs on in a deep freeze of personal protocol, despite the respective unhappiness of the partners.

When two Affection Lines of rather intense depth run side by side for a long spread (figure 66, line A) it signifies a duality at work. Often this shows a marriage that is active and strong, although the individuals are leading different, independent lives. Another reading of these two parallel lines is that the person upon whom these lines are found is also having a long-standing affair that rivals the marriage in importance and depth. Proceed with caution upon seeing this marking and do not jump to conclusions. Begin with gentle questions first that ask how much time the two spouses spend together.

When a Line of Marriage droops toward the Line of Heart (figure 66, line B), it often is called the "widow's mark," indicating that the spouse will die. However, it does not say when. It could be read to mean that the spouse will die before the individual, but not until both are in their very late years. It could also be sudden and soon. Unless there are other defined lines which promise ensuing relationships with others, the Widow's Mark almost always means that whenever the loss occurs, this individual will not remarry, or will mourn for a considerable time. Lastly, this drooping line can be a sign that a long marriage itself dies—burns out. After thirty years of marriage people with this line suddenly surprise their kids and split up abruptly; the flame of love has died. You have to be intuitive to pick up on this last implication, although I can attest to seeing it more and more often in recent years.

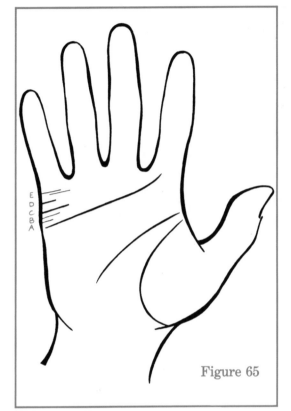

Figure 65

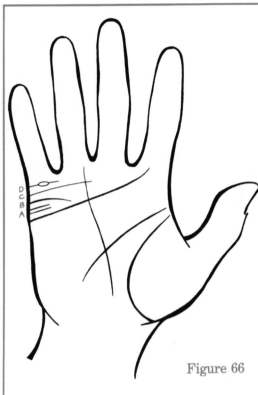

Figure 66

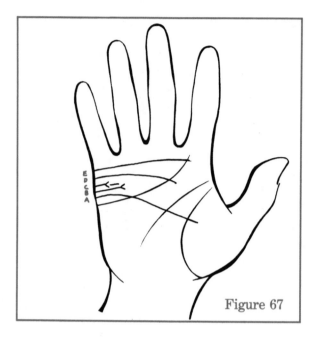

Figure 67

When an Affection Line is long and actually touches the Line of Sun (figure 66, line C), this is considered to be very lucky. The marriage is blessed with great social success and the individual probably has married up in money or class. An alternate meaning is that the spouse, or loved one, has greatly aided the career of the person who bears this line. When the line appears on a man, you'll know immediately that there is a great woman behind his greatness, and vice versa when it appears on the hand of a woman.

When a Line of Affection has an island in it (figure 66, line D), the standard interpretation is that a scandal clouds or rocks the marriage. I take exception to this reading, having found that it more often reveals a couple who has drifted apart from one another during part of the marriage. The rift could be caused by external incompatible interests or by real emotional upsets. The quarrels are strong enough to cause an isolating effect—a distancing—but this is only a island and can be overcome later in the marriage as the two regain their unity.

If the line is so long that it crosses the Lines of Heart, Head, and Life, and terminates in the Mount of Venus (figure 67, line A), a very complicated and rare situation exists. It can be a sign of a powerful, energetic, driving marriage, with erotic fireworks. More frequently this Line of Marriage depicts a slew of problems. With all that energy the partners can be combative and may be led into infidelities. The wedding ring can become the proverbial wrestling ring!

When the line forks at the end (figure 67, line B) the classic reading is of a divorce, with each spouse going off in a separate direction. *Should a line form after the fork* (figure 67, line C), it indicates that the two were able to use their separation to repair their relationship. This can be a hopeful sign that all is not lost.

When the line is long and droops into the quadrangle between the Line of Heart and Head (figure 67, line D), you'll know that this person has a rare and potent relationship. Here the powers of head and heart come together to make this marriage a constant source of idealistic inspiration.

When the line *runs across the base of the other mounts* (figure 67, line E), the implication is that the marriage assumes an element of private hysteria. There are characteristics here which make me think of Lady Macbeth—someone with a single-minded obsession for power and the willingness to push the marriage ahead to obtain that power. You'll observe this pathway more than any of the other long lines originating on the Mount of Mercury. In all cases there will be a powerful marriage that operates on many levels between the two partners. Sometimes these mutual energies can support the marriage with an outcome of great career success beneficial to both. In other contexts, however, the involvement may be corrupted; when ambitious attempts at upward mobility overwhelm the original love, the individual's destiny can be as tragic as that of Macbeth. When encountering this line, do recognize the strength of will to succeed, to have all levels of a marriage work in big impressive ways. At the same time, there will be an inherent competitiveness that must be balanced for a truly happy and lasting union.

If you have any questions about the success of any relationship line, conduct a simple test. First, to the very best of your ability, gauge the timing of the line that is under scrutiny. Then look at the Lines of Fate and Sun to see if the time of the Affection Line is complemented by any particular change, either positively or negatively, in either or both of these lines. These correlations can often be found between the various lines in the hand. For example, should you decide that the relationship represented by the given Affection Line occurs at age thirty-five, and you also perceive that the individual has a spurt of growth at age thirty-five as marked on the Line of Sun, then you have hit on a positive correlation that the relationship is progressing well. Mind you, when considering the same Marriage Line, if the Fate Line breaks or is weakened at age thirty-five, you've found a negative correlation—a relationship indicated by the Affection Line will be a hindrance to other pursuits.

MARRIAGE LINES AND THE MOUNT OF NEPTUNE

The Mount of Neptune, the sea, is another source for the inscription of relationship lines. These lines must come from the Mount of Neptune or the outer edge of the Plain of Mars, flow in, and merge with the Line of Fate. Some palmists are convinced that these are the only true Lines of Marriage and that all others are only lines of affection.

I believe that every one of the Affection Lines, regardless of placement in any of the five areas we are discussing, has the potential to be a strong line of union or marriage. This illustrates why palmistry is an art rather than a science—all signs are expressed through different interpretations. Consider another interpretive art: singing. A song sung by one artist sounds exquisite. Sung by another singer, this same song is terrible. Same song, different interpretations. This is likewise true of palmistry. One reader finds all the ambiguity, all the truth, all the soulful growth. Another reader misses these elements, finding only heartache, with none of the transformation. That is why even in the field of medicine we have doctors who are healers of the whole person, healers who take in all signs of mind, heart, body, and spirit. And then we have doctors who simply dispense pills. The former is a higher practitioner of an art, the latter is a mere mechanic, one who "paints by numbers."

The basic palmistry principles used to read the Nepture Lines as relationship lines come from the idea that the percussion side of the hand represents influence from outside the family. *When the line joins with the Line of Fate*, a partnership is formed. This type of union is read often by astrologers as occurring in the seventh house. These are partners who show the effect of a mentor or another person who

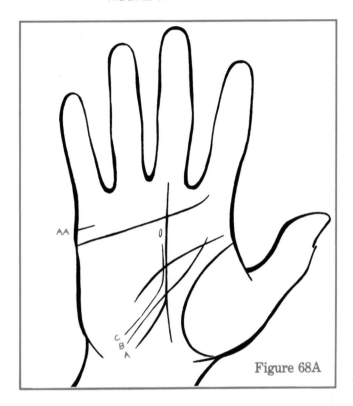

Figure 68A

has altered the individual in either a positive or negative way. The person changes for better or for worse depending on how the Fate Line intersects the Neptune Line.

Use the example shown by the Neptune Line A on Figure 68A. The *point of intersection on the Fate Line* happens at age twenty-two, a fairly easy age to gauge. Again, when you have a correlating union line, as on the Mount of Mercury, you'll have an "A-A" agreement and you are assured of a true union or marriage. If Line A was alone on the hand without the corresponding A-A agreement, then the strong possibility would still exist that the relationship was a marriage, though not necessarily a partner or mentor. Only by asking the individual something about the relationship would you be able to ascertain or predict related events.

Another variation of trouble is seen (figure 68A, line B) *when a Neptune Line passes through a Fate Line without a break and continues up to cross the Line of Head into the outer reaches of the Mount of Jupiter (line B), winding up in the grand quadrangle.* This is a marriage line with the unfortunate implication that the individual sacrifices for a spouse or is sacrificed by that spouse for something or someone else.

Line C (figure 68A) is a line of a very serious relationship in which deepest love is permanent between the partners but which does not ever lead to marriage, or not until after a considerable wait. The key to this interpretation is that *the Neptune Line never formally joins with the Fate Line.* There is an old wives' tale that says if the line ends near an island (end line C), the relationship will end in scandal. I haven't seen this very often and I don't become very alarmed when I do. After all, what was once scandal is today what all the neighbors are doing anyway!

Line A on figure 68B shows *a line that cuts across the Line of Fate and stops.* That the line does not join with the Fate Line is the clue to what we can expect. This is not a union, it is only an encounter. Here is the boy from the big city who comes to town for the summer and gets his way with the small-town girl. Or perhaps this indicates an older woman who introduces a younger man to love and heartache. However the archetype manifests itself, the reading always boils down to a love that is not a true union and therefore does not work. It is best if the Fate Line doesn't break, for then the individual surfaces from these "rites of passage" without huge disruptions in the rest of his or her life. Should the line break, expect a story of trauma and drama.

Line B of figure 68B, which *crosses the Line of Fate and ends under or in a Mystic Cross* (X) is a sign of deep spiritual love with a willingness for great personal sacrifice in order to live a life that upholds spiritual ideals. It is sometimes called the "Line of the Martyr"—but martyrs are hard to find in the Twentieth Century!

Line C of figure 68B is a line of a person who at age thirty-nine or forty experiences a deep love and union. It is included to help you test your ability at judging timing on a hand and also to show that these lines can originate in the grand quadrangle. There is no age at which it is impossible for these love lines to happen; love's lines start where the love starts.

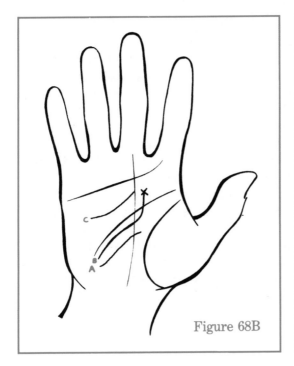

Figure 68B

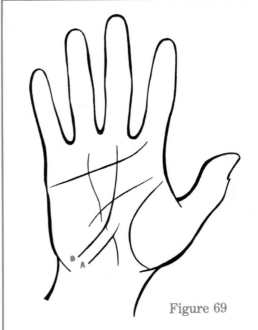

Figure 69

If the Fate Line breaks and the Neptune Line passes on through it (figure 69, line A), this is a negative omen. Here is a person who enters the life of the individual and is somehow destructive to the individual. It might be the playboy who dumps his new bride, the young bride who writes the military serviceman a 'Dear John' letter, or the seductive college English professor who wants to teach more than poetry to his pupil. Such breaking lines always suggest a rough experience, often a broken vow of the heart, or marriage.

The breaking of the Line of Fate by a Neptune Line (figure 69, line A) is a negative sign that the person is involved in a bad relationship which radically changes the perception of fate and reality in a destructive way. But there still may be reason to rejoice. On this hand there is hope (figure 69A, line B) in the appearance of a second Neptune Line joining up with the broken Fate Line. This is an indication that the individual learns and grows from the negative experience, and consequently meets a new partner who makes for a wonderful relationship. Just how wonderful the relationship is over time will be shown by the Line of Sun and quality of the line at the time of the union. This configuration tells the whole story: falling in love, getting hurt, learning, falling in love again, making it work, enjoying life. "Transformation leads to regeneration," was what one old palmist said, and I believe him.

Please don't be alarmed, as some of my close associates have been, if you do not have any Neptune Lines to point up a great union in your hand. As I have stressed before, these lines occur in only one of the five places on the palm where love can be seen. Everyone has activity on at least two areas, if not on all five. What counts above all is that your feelings and ideas about love are explored for growth and personal self-realization.

LINES ON THE MOUNT OF VENUS

A few noted palmists look to the Mount of Venus for Lines of Marriage. My personal thinking is that the line on this Mount are lines of physical attractions, affairs, body chemistry. The third point of view, held by the famed Chinese palmist, Kwok Man Po, whom I was fortunate enough to meet in Hawaii, says that both union lines and attraction lines can be read on the Mount of Venus. Let's take a closer look.

Figure 70 shows five varieties of *affection* or relationship lines on the Mount of Venus. Line A is considered to be a Line of Marriage. It is a *long line inside the Inner Line of Life,* which indicates a long and lasting affection. The clue to its nature is its length; in its support to the life there will be a constancy of love and commitment.

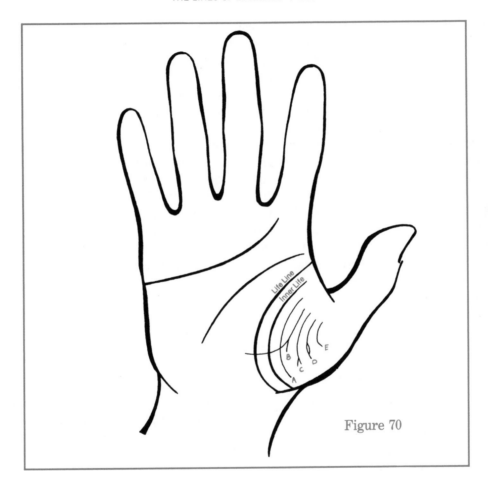

Figure 70

When the line is *short* (figure 70, line B), it is an affair line. *If the line is short and has a fork which cuts across the Line of Life*, it is a sign that the affair will bring dishonor or gossip that will affect the life.

Line C of figure 70 ends in a *fork*, suggesting a relationship that ends in separation or divorce. Line E is a line that is *short and whose end pulls back from the Line of Life*. This indicates an affair that fizzles out in a fading away of interest.

The Chinese palmists interpret Figure 70, Line D, *the line with an island*, to mean that both partners will commit adultery! Imagine. I suggest that this might just mean that they are separated by different schedules or interests. Still, the Chinese reading is more flavorful!

While you may feel certain reservations about the definitions given to these lines, they are good indicators of one's sex drive. As affection lines they often reveal the physical drive this person brings to a marriage. A solid marriage line on Mercury and a strong physical union line on Venus can make for a sexually strong marriage. A weak marriage line on Mercury and several physical attraction lines like B or E of figure 70 and you may well suspect that the individual will have to seek sex outside of the marriage. This is yet another illustration of how relationship lines on different areas of the palm must all be considered to gain the clearest picture.

RELATIONSHIP LINES ON THE THUMB

At the base of the thumb between Venus and Athena, there is a ring commonly called the Ring of Family (figure 71, line F). Certain Gypsy traditions hold that additional rings above this Ring of Family are marriage rings (figure 71, line A). More specifically, they are thought to be rings which show marriage that produce children. Lines which are not rings around Athena (figure 71, line B) are considered to be nonbearing relationships.

While Gypsies are famous for practicing the art of palmistry, this approach to the second phalange of the thumb should not be followed as gospel. Very little literature deals with this possibility. When I first encountered the idea while working at a fortune-telling tent next to some Gypsies at the L.A. County Fair, I found this relationship line to be helpful, though not fail-safe. In a situation in which no other lines on the hand yield a meaningful indication of how many childbearing relationships exist for the individual, this is the place to look. In addition, the phalange of

Athena represents will. To sustain a marriage takes a great deal of will; consequently I found the Gypsy reading of these rings to be quite useful when at a loss for signs from other lines. However, please look first for other lines on the hand before resorting to the thumb alone.

SPECIAL MARKS

There are a few special marks which are worth our attention. A cross on the Mount of Jupiter is a sign of leadership and a very proud and passionate marriage, and an individual who has risen to a high goal of social and romantic calling. The timing of the marriage is gauged by the closeness of the cross to the Heart Line. In the case of two crosses (figure 71, C & D), C would be the first marriage, D would be the later marriage. Power is always involved as fertile Jupiter combines great leadership and the desire to leave a large "kingdom" to the family, or to create a dynasty. This is an exciting mark, even if it often signals an inflated ego.

When a triangle is formed on a line of the Mount of Venus (line H on figure 71), it is a sign of a very lucky, unusually happy union, regardless of whether the line upon which the triangle forms is long or short.

A trident (figure 71, mark E) at the end of a line of Mercury is a sign of a very ambitious marriage. These individuals will take on great tasks as a couple. The trident of Neptune in this configuration brings tremendous power of vision and insight to both parties, not to mention respective charm and the will to achieve. Remember that Neptune was called the "shaker" of the earth and you can imagine why this couple will be expected to take the world by storm together. That is, of course, within their sphere of influence!

LINES OF CHILDREN

A quick estimation of the number of children can be made by examining the Relationship Lines on Mercury for small vertical lines (figure 71, line G) that radiate off the deepest of the union lines.

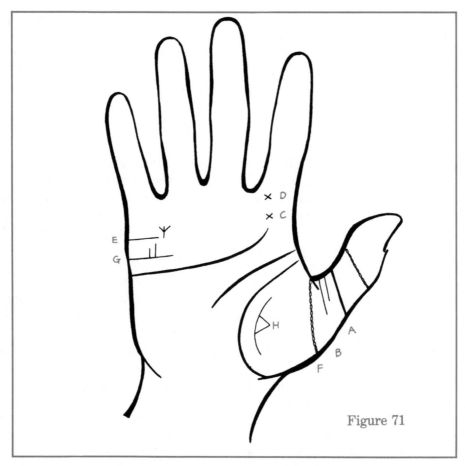

Figure 71

Reading the Lines of Children is much like weather forecasting. Some days you're on the money, some days you're off the target. Once, while working at a charity function, I read a palm of a very nice lady who inquired about her children. I saw five. She laughed and informed me that she was a nun. Naturally,I felt quite foolish until, with much grace, she told me that five was accurate. She was married symbolically to Christ and had adopted five children who were as much of a family to her as if she had borne them herself. My reading had pleased her, and I was equally impressed that she had accepted adopted children as her very own. The point to note in this encounter is that the children lines coming off Relationship Lines on Mercury do not necessarily reveal biological children. Rather, these lines indicate a mental attitude of the individual toward children, be they nephews, nieces, students, other people's children, or even pets and plants. Look to the children lines on Mercury to show how nurturing this person is to all living things.

You can assume that when you see a great many lines, you have met someone who likes living creatures of all kinds. You can further assess which lines indicate actual children and how many are shown by looking at the ones that touch the deeper Relationship Lines and counting them only. Do use your intuition here. If some of the children lines are very faint, exclude them. Of those that you decide are strong, examine them for length and thickness. Thickness equals boys, thinness is for girls. The longest line, whether "boy" or "girl," tells which is the favored child.

You have now seen a wide sampling of the places that Lines of Marriage or Union can be found on the hand and the many forms they can take. These lines are possibly the most frequently discussed and most scrutinized on the palm. Marriage is such a vital topic; it represents a lasting, legal, and totally intimate relationship with another human being.

I want to close this chapter by giving you the best advice a palmist can give about marriage and compatibility. After years of experience, let me urge my readers to memorize the chapters on the Lines of Heart and Head. These two lines and their configurations will serve you more in terms of seeing the inner nature and the core sensibility of the partner than any other markings. It can be said that the heart shapes the head, and the head shapes the heart. The highest tribute to human will is that we can choose whom to love. We do not choose because of a primal, instinctive battle during mating season when the moon is full and in which the most powerful beast wins the beloved. The human species has reached the level in evolution at which we can make up our own minds about whom we love and with whom we will have children. It's as if Mother Nature said, "Okay, let's see what love and the human mind can do." The challenge is for us to discover which is best—if choice can make for a transcendent species, or if the instinctive mating rituals of the animal world should be our mode as well. I vote for free choice: love and insight will bring us to a better day.

10

MINOR LINES
and SPECIAL
S I G N S

T he minor lines and special signs are uncommon. Not every hand will bear any of these markings. They indicate a special talent or aptitude and need careful consideration. Specific skill areas or psychological characteristics symbolized by a special marking may reveal a potentially important personality trait. For example, if you like mysticism or deep religious discussion, look for a palm with the mystic cross. Want to talk all night about owning your own business, look for the Entrepreneurial Line. Want a sixties' pothead radical who is now a healthnut yuppie, look for Neptune's Rocking Horse.

In considering a person as a prospective love interest, it's a good idea to study the following examples to be able to spot the most powerful of these unique marks. Look upon them as spices on palmistry's shelf. Know how they affect your romantic taste and date accordingly.

MINOR LINES

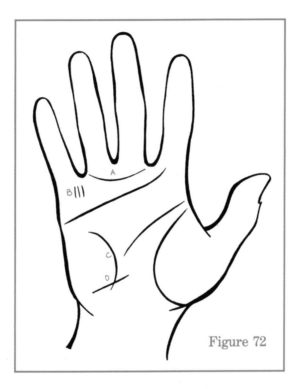

Figure 72

Girdle of Venus (figure 72, line A) indicates high sensitivity, artistic temperament, great visual imagination, a hyperaware form of charisma.

Chiron's Bundle (figure 72, line B) indicates a teacher, healer, or good Samaritan who seeks to act for the good of humanity.

Diana's Bow (figure 72, line C) indicates a keen sense of intuition, sharp instincts, heightened sensitivity, and excellent ESP.

Diana's Arrow (figure 72, line D) indicates a tendency to compulsive activity, high energy for short periods, and possible allergies or "nervous tics."

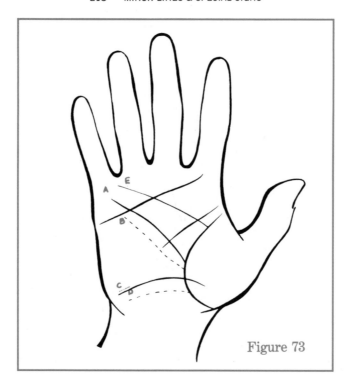

Figure 73

Neptune's Rocking Horse (figure 73, lines C or D) indicates a high/low, up/down, escapist, or spaced-out personality who seeks release through a variety of ways: sex, drugs, mental fantasies, gurus, gambling, celibacy, booze, religion, or abstinence. This mark indicates a swing in activities and attitudes that can create a workaholic as well as an alcoholic, a dreamer, or inventor.

Line of Mercury (figure 73, lines A or B) indicates good business sense, the ability to communicate and negotiate with real vigor—also can mean ulcers and nervous quirks due to business pressure.

Entrepreneurial Line (figure 73, line E) indicates a drive to have one's own business, to be the leader, to be boss. In corporate structures, these individuals negotiate special incentive packages so that they are paid for their productivity.

SPECIAL SIGNS

△ △   *Triangle*—indicates a special talent or time period on the palm. Recognition, growth, and opportunity are to be found when the triangle is present. Consider the point of the hand where it is found: on Jupiter, for example, a lucky personality; on the Line of Life, a lucky period of time.

Ψ Ψ Ψ   *Trident*—indicates a magnetic quality, depending on where it is found. On Mount of Luna, for example, the imagination will have a compelling quality, a great artistic talent, or the ability to shape ideas; on Mount of Mercury, a great orator.

⅄ ✕ *Cross*—indicates a deep and challenging drive. It is the product of a conflict that can be evaluated by where on the hand it appears. On Saturn, for example, it represents a "moral" personality that may want to control you.

✳ *Star*—indicates an unusual talent that will bring success in the area where it appears.

◇ *Diamond*—indicates inventiveness, sharp perception, and the energy to get a job done. Brings success.

)(*Crescent*—indicates intuitive feelings, a special insight, or special insight relative to the area of the hand in which it occurs.

□ *Square*—indicates the ability to survive, to get through tough times, to receive protection in either sprirtual or material matters.

Grille—indicates nervousness, anxiety, hypersensitivity, or a touchy personality.

Mystic Cross—indicates a deep spiritual or transcendental potential for inner vision and faith. These individuals can perceive the underlying unity of the universe and the need to experience a union of mind with this greater whole.

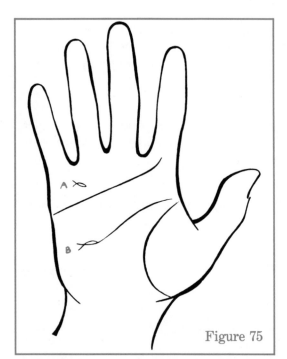

Figure 75

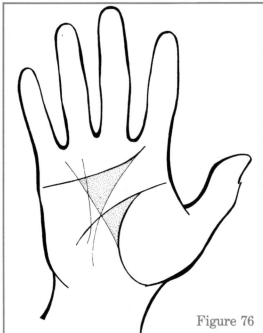

Figure 76

Fish (figure 75)—indicates great faith and vision, brings hope and inspiration to the area of the hand where found.

Butterfly (figure 76)—indicates a person who is a good team builder, a good disseminator of ideas, a catalyst.

11

IS WHAT YOU FORESEE WHAT YOU GET?

W hen the party is over, the hospitality suite is closing, the ESP/Psychic Fair is wrapping up, and the private consultation is finished, that's when the palmist faces a few stragglers who want to "talk." And they always ask, "How true is all this, anyway?"

This is a legitimate inquiry. What can be foreseen by the lines in the hand raises the natural question of the accuracy of palmistry and the role of determinism: Is fate or free will the ruler of man? If lines on the hand can tell something about how your life may turn out, does that mean you have no free will? I don't think so. We are here to exercise free will. The answer to this query might be best explained by using a game of chance as a formula.

During my days working at *VIVA* Magazine, I used to play a lot of backgammon, both for money stakes and in tournaments. I got to know many of the greats of the game. Often I'd get sidetracked at tournaments reading palms—it was fun, casual, and a great way to meet a lot of interesting characters. The point is that backgammon is a very profound game, in many ways a more profound model for life than chess. In chess the good player will beat the weaker player most of the time. In back-gammon, however, an inferior player can beat a good player in any given single game at any given time, because of the roll of the dice. The dice are what make backgammon the most instructive training for dealing with the realities of life. The task is to play intelligently what the dice give you, time after time, so that as the rolls of the dice continue, the better player gains an advantage by making strong moves, even with bad dice.

What has this got to do with life or palmistry, let alone relationships? Isn't life a lot like a roll of the dice? Price of admission: one roll of the genetic code when the sperm enters the egg at the moment of conception. Yet even in the face of such a determined destiny, I honestly and sincerely believe that the essence of man's nature is free will.

Allow me to return to backgammon and my use of this great game to explain free will and determinism. Everyone receives certain qualities—their height, girth, eye strength, coordination, mental skills. These are the rolls of your dice in an allegorical backgammon game. Still it is how you play these rolls (the hand you've been dealt) that is important. It is how you capitalize on yourself—on what God gave you—that makes a difference.

Life is getting a grip on your real talents and making them work for you. This is why people with the same disabilities or hardships respond in different ways. Some succumb to their problems, while some throw away their crutches and become champions. These people are playing the same dice differently; they have taken on a different mental attitude toward the "givens" in their lives, and they have refused to "give up."

The lesson here is not to look on the lines of the hand in deterministic terms, for the lines on the hand change! The initial lines represent the "opening roll," the potential of the individual. The next step is to see how much the individual can make of it. Look at the hands of young children and you will see how the lines change as they move from infancy to late adolescence—the hand has a tendency to stop changing as the personality is set. The sad part is that few people really do change beyond their late teen years, despite their capacity to do so.

With your new knowledge of palmistry you are prepared to look in a metaphysical way for a lover/partner. Love is the honoring of a reciprocal affection between two open and vulnerable individuals whose inner bond commits them to higher goals. Love is a celebration: two souls have found each other, and are joined together in the cosmic dance.

The Personal Index given at the end of the first section of this book is an excellent way to evaluate a person's compatibility level. Note how accurate palmistry is or isn't on different types of people you know. After a few times of testing this method on a variety of friends you will start to fine tune your approach. Then you will be able to spot the bad apples before even putting them in your shopping cart!

Really, all you need to discover is what points of palmistry are accurate for you. As Grandmother Harris used to say, "If it works for you, it works for you." And palmistry has worked for ages. It can reveal your inner nature and how to respect yourself. It can show you what you expect in love. Inventory yourself, and use the Personal Index to augment your insights into others. Keep an eye on your goal of a meaningful relationship. Don't repeat negative dating patterns. Make sharp and meaningful choices about whom you wish to spend time with. Before you know it, you'll have *romance on your hands*.

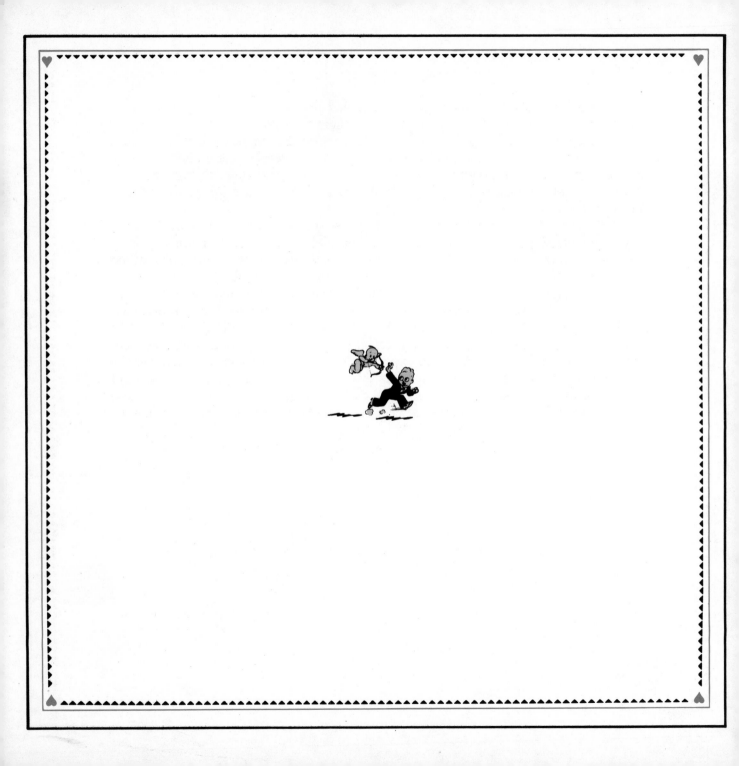